AK47

The Complete Kalashnikov Family of Assault Rifles

PALADIN PRESS
BOULDER, COLORADO

DUNCAN LONG

AK47: The Complete Kalashnikov Family of Assault Rifles
by Duncan Long

Copyright 1988 by Duncan Long

ISBN 0-87364-477-8

Printed in the United States of America

Published by Paladin Press, a division of
Paladin Enterprises, Inc., P.O. Box 1307,
Boulder, Colorado 80306, USA.
(303) 443-7250

Direct inquiries and/or orders to the above address.

PALADIN, PALADIN PRESS, and the "horse head" design
are trademarks belonging to Paladin Enterprises and
registered in United States Patent and Trademark Office.

Contents

Also by Duncan Long:

AR-7 Super Systems
The AR-15/M16: A Practical Guide
AR-15/M16 Super Systems
Automatics: Fast Firepower, Tactical Superiority
Combat Ammo of the 21st Century
Combat Revolvers: The Best (and Worst) Modern Wheelguns
Combat Rifles of the 21st Century: Futuristic Firearms for
    Tomorrow's Battlefields
Making Your AR-15 into a Legal Pistol
The Mini-14: The Plinker, Hunter, Assault, and Everything
    Else Rifle
Mini-14 Super Systems
Modern Ballistic Armor: Clothing, Bomb Blankets, Shields,
    Vehicle Protection . . . Everything You Need to Know
Modern Sniper Rifles
The Poor Man's Fort Knox: Home Security with Inexpensive
    Safes
Powerhouse Pistols: The Colt 1911 and Browning Hi-Power
    Sourcebook
The Ruger .22 Automatic Pistol: Standard/Mark I/Mark II
    Series
Streetsweepers: The Complete Book of Combat Shotguns
The Sturm, Ruger 10/22 Rifle and .44 Magnum Carbine
The Terrifying Three: Uzi, Ingram, and Intratec Weapons
    Families

Acknowledgments

◉ —————————————————————————— ◉

Thanks must go to the manufacturers and importers who graciously loaned firearms to me to test during the writing of this book, and to the many companies that sent sample accessories and products to inspect and test out. A number of companies, including Federal Cartridge Company, Olin/Winchester, Hansen Cartridge Company, and PMC, supplied me with numerous types of ammunition to test out the firearms in this book. Hercules and Hodgdon provided "CARE packages" of powder to reload empty brass.

Thanks also to the fine people at Paladin Press for the expert work they continue to do in transforming my rough manuscripts into beautifully crafted books.

A thank-you should also go to my dad for his work in processing many of the photos in the book; and the usual very special thanks to Maggie, Kristen, and Nicholas for their help and patience.

Chapter 1

◉ ———————————————————————— ◉

History of the Kalashnikov Rifles

Russia was nearly the first country to develop the assault rifle, but history gives the achievement to Nazi Germany instead during the last years of World War II. The near miss occurred in 1916. Plans for a lightweight rifle were created by Vladimir Grigorevich Federov (whose name is also sometimes spelled "Fyodora" in the West), one of the Czar's arms designers. Federov had proposed the concept of a lightweight self-loading rifle in several of his books, and in the early 1900s, he actually created several working prototypes.

Most of the armies of the world were working on self-loading infantry rifle projects following the introduction of the automatic pistol and machine gun to the battlefield, but Federov's idea of using a low-powered rifle round to minimize recoil and wear and tear on the firearm was a first. Federov's choice of rounds was the Japanese 6.5mm Meiji 30 cartridge, an intermediate round with less power than most contemporary military rifle cartridges. Thus, when Federov's "new" 7.62x 54mmSR cartridge was used in his firearm, the result was more or less an assault rifle by modern standards (albeit a bit long and heavy).

The Federov Avtomat was very like today's modern assault rifle. Had communist bureaucrats spent less time hassling the rifle's inventor and more on developing the weapon, Russia might have been decades ahead of others in small-arms development.

Federov's rifle is generally known today as the *Federov Avtomat*. A limited number were created in 1916 and used by Russian forces during World War I. This has led to speculation among historians as to whether the Russian rifle might have inspired the creation of the German assault rifles during the next world war.

Unfortunately for the Soviets, Federov didn't fit in well with the party bureaucrats who took over after the Czar was overthrown. Although Federov had thrown in his lot with the communists during the 1917 revolution, he still held many capitalist ideas, like paying skilled machinists and designers more than common laborers on the assembly line. Federov was even jailed for a short time because of his views and seems to have worked in constant conflict with the Soviet government. This, coupled with a lack of raw materials, poor decision making (usually by "people's committees"), and lack of skilled workers and machinery, made it nearly impossible to produce many of the new rifles even after the Avtomat was adopted by the communist military and production work was supposed to go ahead at top capacity.

Despite the fact that the first rifles were made in 1916, the Main Artillery Commission didn't give the go-ahead to start production of the Federov Avtomat until 1919. The numbers of the Avtomats produced give some idea of the factory conditions which existed during the time. Even with an engineering team and at least 100 workers, the small factory producing the rifles managed to manufacture only 50 rifles per month at peak production. Over the six years the plant operated, it's believed that only slightly more than 3,000 rifles were produced before the operation was terminated.

In addition to being hard to manufacture, the Federov Avtomat was sensitive to dirt and abuse in the field. In 1925, the communist leaders discontinued its manufacture and started a search for a more suitable rifle. Unfortunately, the decision makers decided that the new rifle should use the old 7.62x54mmR cartridge used in Russian bolt-action rifles, probably to take advantage of a large stockpile of ammunition which would be practically useless if a new cartridge were adopted. This old rimmed cartridge proved awkward to use in semiautomatic action and was powerful enough to guarantee that any rifle based on it would be hard to control and prone to parts breakage.

After a series of tries, a new infantry rifle designed by Sergei Gavrilovich Simonov was adopted as the AVS36 (*Avtomaticheskaya Vintovka Simonova obrazets 1936*). As one would expect, this weapon proved unsatisfactory because of its cartridge. Soviet planners were soon looking for a replacement after fewer than 40,000 of the rifles were produced.

Three new self-loading designs were submitted for trials; one was another design from Simonov while the others were from N.V. Rukavishnikov and F. V. Tokarev. Of these three, the Tokarev rifle proved to be the most reliable and was adopted in 1939 as the SVT38

(*Samozaryadnaya Vintovka Tokareva* –Self-loading Tokarev–1938).

The Russian SVT38 was very heavy, quite complicated, and hard to manufacture. This, coupled with its too-powerful cartridge, made it a rather poor weapon for the Soviets.

All was not well with the SVT38. Although the rifle functioned well during testing, it was very heavy and also quite complicated, which made it hard to manufacture. In addition to its manufacturing problems, the SVT38 proved less durable in the field than had been hoped. In an effort to alleviate some of these problems, the rifle's design was modified slightly and the firearm was redesignated the SVT40. As with the SVT38, a sniper version of the SVT40 was created by mounting a scope on select rifles. Short carbine versions of the SVT40 were also made, as well as a selective-fire version, the AVT40.

The SVT40 was a slightly stronger rifle. The major design changes consisted of a simplified handguard and a change in cleaning rod position so that it was carried under the barrel rather than in the long groove down the side of the rifle as with the SVT38. The muzzle brake of initial SVT40s had six narrow slots cut in it while later models had two large baffle cuts –again apparently to cut down on machining steps. These improvements did little to speed up production and made the firearm only marginally more reliable. The Soviets were soon looking for a new gun to replace the SVT40.

At this point, the Soviet military decision makers finally decided to adopt a reduced-power round. One would like to think that Federov's idea of using a round with reduced power in a semiauto rifle had finally sunk in. In fact, it is more likely that the success of the U.S. M1 Carbine and German assault rifles brought about this change in Soviet thinking.

The U.S. M1 Carbine made its debut in World War II. Though the carbine's round proved to be a bit anemic for combat, the millions of M1 Carbines which American factories churned out in short order had to have made Soviet bureaucrats envious.

The M1 Carbine made its debut in World War II. Although originally slated for use by personnel who normally carried a .45 pistol, the M1 Carbine ended up being deployed much more widely among U.S. troops. Though its round proved a bit anemic for combat, the millions of M1 Carbines which American factories churned out in short order must have made Soviet bureaucrats envious as their factories chugged out SVTs with alarming slowness.

The German work that took place during the late 1930s might have had a great influence on Soviet decision making as well. The Germans had been working toward the creation of small selective-fire rifles chambered for a small round for some time. The actual introduction of the new battle rifles was slow in coming, but it is possible that the Soviets learned of the German work through their spy network.

By 1943, the German's first assault rifle, designated *Maschinen Pistole* (Machine Pistol—the same words used by the German military to describe its submachine guns), was seeing limited use with an early version, the Haenel Mkb42 (*Maschinenkarabiner* – Machine Carbine – 1942), having been used against the Soviets as early as 1942.

The new German rifles were designed to be easily manufactured. They used sheet-metal stampings for the receiver, had a detachable 30-round magazine, and were simple to field strip and operate. As the end of the war neared, the final version of the German assault rifle was designated the *Sturmgewehr* StG44. Although large numbers of the StG44 were never created, some fell into American and Russian hands following the war and undoubtedly influenced both countries' arms design in later years; they served as the basis of Spain's CETME rifles and Heckler & Koch's G3 series of rifles and submachine guns.

During World War II, Germany produced what many consider the first of the modern assault rifles. One of the best of these was the MP44, which was redesignated the StG44.

Just how much influence the German and American rifle designs had on the Soviets is unknown, but it is known that the Russians started a search for an intermediate round of their own sometime in the early 1940s. By 1943, the USSR had adopted a cartridge designed by N. M. Elizarov and B. V. Semin. The new short round was to have a bullet of the same diameter as the previous Soviet rifle round. Possibly this was a manufacturing expedient since bullets for the new round could be produced on existing equipment. The new 7.62x39mm round was designated the M43. Unlike the powerful rimmed rifle cartridge which had plagued the designs of the AVS36, SVT38, and SVT40, the new round had less power, was shorter, and was rimless –tailor-made for a modern self-loading rifle. At this point, a new rifle was needed for the round and word went out to Soviet designers.

Simonov was waiting in the wings, as it were, with a rifle he had apparently started developing after he first heard of the problems of the SVT38. This new rifle was based on an antitank rifle, the PTRS, which Simonov had created for the Soviet military.

Unfortunately for the Soviets, the new rifle was a bit of a throwback. Simonov's rifles had a fixed magazine rather than a detachable box; while it could be loaded from stripper clips of ammunition, this process was not as quick as a box magazine and limited the rifle's ammunition capacity. Furthermore, although the reduced power of the M43 round made controlled automatic fire possible, Simonov's rifle offered only semiauto fire and the total weight of the firearm was rather heavy. A backward-looking, non-removable folding bayonet was permanently mounted on the barrel of the already-heavy rifle.

Despite these shortcomings, the Soviets made a small number of the rifles and sent them to the Byelorussian front in 1944 for field testing. The rifles proved to be very good in combat and were well liked by the troops. After a few changes in the basic design, the rifle was adopted as the SKS45 (*Samozaryadnyi Karabin sistemi Simonova obrazets* 1945).

The SKS45 was apparently a stop-gap weapon which marginally filled the need for a rifle chambered for the M43 round; it prevented a long wait until a suitable rifle design could be developed from scratch.

Although the SKS45 was of a rather backward-looking design, the basic rifle has been adopted by other communist countries, with large numbers being used by the Chinese as a sort of home guard weapon. The Chinese version is nearly identical to the Soviet design except for a spike bayonet rather than a blade type and is designated the Type 56 Carbine—a bit confusing, since the Chinese Type 56 Rifle is a copy of the AK47. It appears that the Chinese have taken the basic design of the SKS45 one step ahead by placing a detachable box magazine on some of their carbines. These new rifles are currently offered for sale in the United States. If the rifle is actually a modified SKS45 (the rifle was unavailable for examination at the time of this writing), it would appear that this long-overdue modification has created a somewhat handier rifle from the basic Simonov design.

It is a bit of a mystery as to why the Soviets adopted the SKS45 and then quickly chose yet another rifle to replace it several years later. It would appear that the SKS45 was a stopgap weapon which marginally filled the need for a rifle chambered for the M43 and—being available—prevented a long wait until a suitable design could be developed from scratch.

The weapon which replaced the SKS45 was created by an army officer named Mikhail Timofeyevich Kalashnikov, a man whose personal history is the stuff of which legends are made. Born in 1919, Kalashnikov had the Russian equivalent of a high school degree and worked for the Turkestan-Siberian Railroad system until he was drafted into the Soviet army in 1938. In the army, Kalashnikov became fascinated with the operation of firearms and an apparently latent genius for mechanical invention was awakened in him. One of Kalashnikov's superiors noted this interest and enrolled him in an armorer's training course.

In addition to gaining basic armorer skills, Kalashnikov became a tank driver, and soon invented several devices for use in the vehicles. These inventions helped him gain a number of military promotions as well as a job as technical supervisor in the factory making the inventions he'd created for Soviet tanks. Given Kalashnikov's interest in firearms, the experience of seeing modern machining operations probably later influenced the design of his AK rifles.

In 1941, Kalashnikov was called to active duty and fought in the battle for Bryansk. While there, his tank was hit by a shell and Kalashnikov wound up in a hospital. During his convalescence, he made good use of his time by studying all the firearms books he could get his hands on. Interestingly enough, a copy of V.G. Federov's *Evolution of Small Arms* is said to have had the most profound effect on his thinking.

Because of the seriousness of his arm wound, Kalashnikov was allowed to spend six months on leave after being released from the hospital. He spent this time in his hometown of Alma-Ata designing a submachine gun which a machinist friend, Zhenya Kravchenko, helped him fabricate. Once Kalashnikov had a model of the submachine gun, he took it around to communist officials in Alma-Ata until he found one who was interested in sponsoring him to continue work on the new firearm. This official got Kalashnikov a job in the model shops of the *Moskovsky Aviasionniy Institut* (Moscow Aviation Institute) which, as luck would have it, had been moved to Alma-Ata.

The outcome of Kalashnikov's work was a submachine gun which had little to offer over the PPS which had only just been adopted. But, in showing his model to the Soviet military, Kalashnikov gained the attention of armaments personnel who recognized his talent and offered the young man a job at the military proving ground in Ensk. Kalashnikov quickly accepted.

While at Ensk, Kalashnikov had a chance to meet designers like Simonov, Degtyarev, and others; this undoubtedly proved to be very inspirational as well as educational to the self-taught inventor. Soon Kalashnikov had developed several improvements for Soviet machine guns in addition to other minor design jobs. Most importantly, however, Kalashnikov received a number of the new M43 rounds and was told by colleagues at Ensk that there was a search on for a new rifle chambered for the cartridge. This call for a new rifle inspired Kalashnikov to start work on a firearm based on the M43. By 1944, Kalashnikov had produced a carbine which was tested but rejected in favor of the SKS45.

Soon word got out that a new rifle would be needed to replace the SKS45; Kalashnikov and other Soviet small arms designers again started working on new rifle designs. In 1946, Kalashnikov sent off the drawings for a new gas-operated rifle based on the M43 cartridge to the Main Artillery Commission in Moscow. The committee decided that Kalashnikov's design had merit and gave him the go-ahead to create several test models.

Kalashnikov assembled a small design team which included A. A. Zaytsev, who assisted in making mechanical drawings of the rifle, and Colonel V. S. Demin, who worked on the trigger mechanism, as well as V. A. Khar'kov, V. V. Krupin, and A. D. Kryakushkin, who all did various other tasks. Testing was conducted by V. N. Punshin and N. N. Afanas'yev, with Kalashnikov overseeing all phases of the rifle's development.

From 1946 to 1948, work progressed on the Kalashnikov rifle. As with other modern weapons, progress was slow, with changes having to be made every step of the way. Colonel Demin, for example, had to rework the trigger group at least ten times before it was finally perfected. The trigger group has since changed considerably from one model of the Kalashnikov rifle to another, suggesting that testing and manufacturing techniques continue to dictate changes in this and other minor aspects of the rifle.

Although many in the West like to point out that the Kalashnikov rifles have little in the way of innovation and borrow heavily from weapons like the German StG44 and American M1 Garand and M1 Carbine, the Kalashnikov in fact marks the shift toward a new way of designing firearms which started in the mid-1900s.

In the late 1800s and early 1900s, designing a self-loading rifle or pistol consisted of coming up with an entirely new weapon; trigger group, bolt, and cycling operations were often totally new and displayed the inventor's cunning—or lack thereof—in creating a new firearm. Such a process gives each arms designer the opportunity to exhibit skill and cunning, and gives him a totally new mechanism to patent, but it also means a longer time to develop each weapon and debug it.

By the mid-1900s, a huge number of semiauto and

selective-fire weapons had been created; many were of poor design, while others had good points as well as weaknesses. Because so many operating systems had been generated during this period, designing a wholly new system had become an exercise in futility. At this point, weapons designers were learning that the "quick and dirty" way to create a useful weapon was to reassemble the tested design elements of various firearms into a new configuration.

This sounds easy, but actually requires nearly as much work as creating a unique design; the payoff of this method is that the end result is a firearm which is more reliable than one designed by any one man. All modern firearms are created by this pick-and-choose method; rifles like the AR-15, Daewoo, Beretta, and Enfield are all mixtures of weapons designed many years before.

Consequently, the Kalashnikov rifle has more than a passing resemblance to previous firearms and marks the beginning of the modern era of firearms design. The U.S. M1 Garand and M1 Carbine seem to be the basis of the trigger group and bolt assemblies, while the pistol grip and low barrel/high sight plane bear a striking resemblance to the StG44. Unfortunately, Kalashnikov did not adopt the Garand rifle's excellent safety but rather placed it on the side of the rifle where it could double as a cover for the charging handle. Although his safety was a brilliant feature from a design standpoint, from a human engineering standpoint, it was a terrible failure. Kalashnikov's unhandy, noisy-to-operate safety has proven to be less than ideal in combat.

The safety/selector positions on most versions of the Kalashnikov rifle are: upward position, safe; middle position, automatic fire ("AB" on Soviet rifles); and lower position, semiautomatic fire ("OA" on Soviet guns).

The springs used for the hammer and trigger are made of three-strand cables of smaller spring wire; such springs are no more durable than a large, single-strand spring, but this practice does simplify manufacture. Smaller strands of wire can be used to give the "springiness" of a larger spring which would be harder to work. This spring design was apparently first used on the German MG42.

Kalashnikov rifles are generally thought to be a bit more reliable than others; one reason for this is that they have a large, heavy bolt whose extra momentum allows it to extract and chamber cartridges where rifles with smaller bolts will often jam because of dirt or poorly sized ammunition. This—coupled with the sound Soviet military doctrine of cleaning weapons regularly— is one of the features which has led to the Kalashnikov's reputation of reliability. To ensure that rifles are kept clean, a rigid cleaning rod is mounted below the Kalashnikov's barrel with a small cleaning kit generally found in a storage compartment in the stock.

In 1949, one of Kalashnikov's prototype rifles was accepted as the Soviet Army's AK47 (*Avtomat Kalashnikova obrazets* 1947). Note that the date of the rifle's official acceptance and the date given to the firearm are two years apart; this suggests that perhaps an earlier version of the Kalashnikov met with approval from the Soviet government while acceptance of the final model required working the bugs out of the basic design. Models constructed between 1946 and 1948 were constantly being tested at the Tula test site during this two-year interval.

At the time of the rifle's acceptance, Kalashnikov

left the military and started work at the *Izhevsk Mash-inostroitel'ny Zavod* (Izhevsk Machine Factory). There, he eventually became a senior manager in charge of design and engineering. By the mid-1950s, Kalashnikov apparently had set up at least one OKB (*Opytno-Konstruktorskoe Byuro,* or Experimental Design and Construction Bureau) which continued to develop new versions of the AK47 as well as spinoff machine guns and specialized weapons.

Replacement of the SKS45 by the Kalashnikov was a tedious process with AK47 production going slowly during 1949 and 1950. The first production model had a sheet-metal receiver which is readily distinguished from later models by the lack of any indentations on either side of its receiver. The pistol grip on this first model was in two halves which fastened to a metal extension on the lower rear of the receiver; two metal flanges from the rear of the receiver fastened the wooden stock to the rifle, with one screw on the top and one on the bottom of the stock's forward end. Various sheet-metal parts on the receiver were joined with rivets, and magazines were generally nonribbed and probably somewhat prone to damage in field use.

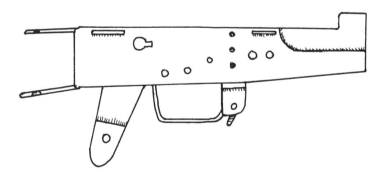

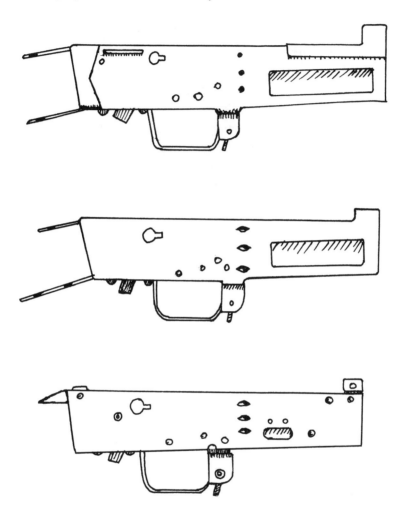

Various models of AK receivers are readily distinguishable by the milling or stamping marks on their receivers and by the method of stock attachment. Facing page: the first sheet-metal version. Top and center: the second and third machined steel receivers. Bottom: the receiver used for the AKM and AK74 series.

In 1951, a second model of the Kalashnikov was introduced which had a milled receiver. The reason for this change is unknown. One theory holds that the sheet-metal receiver of the first AK47s proved to be less durable than expected. Alternatively, military historian Edward Clinton Ezell suggests that the Soviet military-industrial complex may have been strapped for sheet-metal stamping machinery to manufacture other weapons, while steel milling tools sat idle. To get around this problem, the sheet-metal receivers were abandoned and a machined steel receiver substituted on the second model of the AK47, introduced in 1951.

This second AK47 model is readily distinguished by its machined steel receiver and lack of rivets in its side. A long lightening groove is located on each side of the steel receiver ahead of the magazine well; a metal extension at the rear of the receiver holds the stock in place. This receiver extension has two flanges which allow the stock to be fastened to the rifle with two screws; the extension itself is held to the receiver by a single bolt. The one-piece pistol grip is fastened to the receiver via a long bolt in the manner of all subsequent Kalashnikov rifles and spinoff weapons and is usually checkered.

In 1953 or 1954, a third major change was made in the fabrication of the rifle. The receiver extension was abandoned, and a new way of fastening the stock to the receiver was adopted, since the second variation tended to come apart if strain were placed on the stock. This third variation is most readily identified by the absence of the receiver extension; two flanges fasten the stock to the receiver with one screw on top and two on the bottom. The rear sling swivel on the third version was moved from the stock's bottom edge to its side. In addition to other minor changes to strengthen the basic rifle, the magazine now had ribs added to it to make it less susceptible to damage.

The third version of the AK47 with milled receiver and the stock attached directly to the receiver.

A folding stock was also created for the third model. Although the bars of the stock appear to be stampings, they were actually machined from bar stock. This stock latches into place via a spring in the rear of the receiver. To fold the stock, it is released, folded under the rifle, and rotated up to rest alongside either side of the receiver with the butt plate folded up under the fore grip.

In 1959, a new sheet-metal version of the AK47 was fielded. This version, very similar in concept to the original rifle, was engineered to be more durable and was considerably lighter than earlier models. This variation received the designation "AKM" (*Avtomat Kalashnikova sistemi Modernizirovanniy*).

The AKM is readily distinguished by a small indentation on each side of the receiver just over the magazine well and the use of rivets to connect the various parts of the receiver together. On Soviet (as well as most other) models, the upper receiver cover is made of thinner metal than previously; strengthening ribs make it appear quite different from the rounded top of the old AK47s. Other minor outward design changes include lack of porting holes in the gas tube (replaced by holes cut in the edge of the front sight/gas port), raised finger swells in the fore grip, a stock that is more in line with the barrel, and a slanted muzzle compensator to divert gas upward to compensate for muzzle rise during firing. Earlier versions had a muzzle nut over a threaded barrel designed to accept a grenade launcher or possibly a silencer. It is believed that a silencer is made for the Kalashnikov for special use by *Spetsnaz* agents.

Internally, the AKM parts are shaped slightly differently from those of the AK47, and a mechanism was added to the rifle which, according to Soviet training manuals, was designed to reduce the rate of fire. In fact, this device reduces the rate of fire only slightly; it does guarantee that the bolt is fully seated before the weapon fires and therefore acts more as a safety device than rate reducer. (In foreign versions of the AKM, this device is often omitted.)

Materials used in the AKM's furniture (grips and stock) have varied over the course of its manufacture. Laminated wood and plastics of varying colors have been used in Soviet weapons; other communist countries also vary the furniture considerably. It is not uncommon to see rifles with several types or styles of furniture combined on one gun, since grips and stocks are generally interchangeable.

The AK47's folding stock design was used on many AKMs, but the stock bars were made of steel stampings instead of machined bars. A folding-stock rifle is generally designated an AKMS. Many of these stocks are slightly shorter than the original AK47 model, probably to make them easier to use in armored vehicles; they would also undoubtedly be better suited to shorter shooters who might find the standard stock a bit long. A sling swivel is attached to the left of the folding stock where it connects to the receiver on the AKMS.

As in the West, Soviet military decision makers still seemed concerned with ranges of fire not normally encountered in combat when the AKM was designed. Although numerous studies have shown that most combat occurs within 150 yards, with extreme ranges of 300 yards encountered only rarely, the AKM's sights were recalibrated from the already optimistic 800 meters of the AK47 out to a maximum of 1,000 meters. Because of the emphasis on nighttime fighting in Soviet military doctrine, most AKMs also have luminous dots located on their rear sights to aid aiming in the dark. Because virtually all of the communist countries use corrosive ammunition, all models of the AKM have chromed bores and stainless-steel or chrome-coated gas pistons and bolt carriers to minimize corrosion.

Currently, many communist countries use the AKM, with AK47s being used by reserve units and the like. At the time of this writing, most rifles exported to the United States are also of the AKM design, although they are generally called AK47s. Even the "experts" tend to use the term "AK47" as a generic word encompassing both the AK47 and AKM.

The AKM became the basis of other weapons systems, including the RPK LMG (light machine gun); the PK general-purpose machine gun (bipod mount); the PKS medium machine gun (tripod mount); the PKT tank machine gun; and the PKB for armored personnel carriers (more about all these weapons in another chapter).

In the early 1970s, a new 5.45x39.5mm cartridge was developed for use in Soviet small arms. The new round was adopted as the M74 and appears to have been inspired by the U.S. 5.56x45mm combat round. The U.S. .223 Remington, or 5.56x45mm, round had proven to be more effective in combat than the M43, principally because the smaller round broke apart or tumbled on impact, whereas the M43 bullet did neither, causing less serious wounds despite its greater power. This lesson seems to have been taken to heart by Soviet military planners.

The AK74 is nearly identical to the AKM but is chambered for the Soviet 5.45x39 cartridge. The rifle is readily distinguished by its muzzle brake, differently curved magazine, and the horizontal cut in its stock.

The AKM was adapted to use the M74; the new rifle was designated the AK74 (*Avtomat Kalashnikova obrazets* 1974). When first seen by those in the West at Russian May Day parades and by American and British journalists in Afghanistan, the rifles were thought to be used only by specialized units. In fact, the Soviets seem to be replacing all AKM rifles with AK74s; the older guns are apparently being used for reserve units.

As with the AK47 and AKM rifles, the Warsaw Pact countries seem to be moving toward weapons chambered for the new round. Hungary, Poland, and East Germany are all known to be producing such weapons and ammunition at the time of this writing. It is also believed that production of the AK47 and AKM has been discontinued except for export to countries still using the M43, as well as to sporting shooters and collectors in the United States and elsewhere.

The AK74 is basically an AKM with a new bolt/ barrel assembly adapted to the smaller round. Early rifles used non-ribbed, steel-reinforced fiberglass magazines which were nearly identical to late-manufacture AKM magazines except for a different curve to accommodate the M74 cartridge's taper. Later magazines appear to be made of dark ABS plastic; this undoubtedly is better for camouflage, but the new magazine is probably considerably less durable.

The bolt-to-cartridge ratio which helped give the AK47 and AKM their reputation for reliability has actually been increased in the AK74. In order to keep the bolt extractor from pulling through the rim of a hard-to-extract cartridge, the M74 round has a very thick rim. These two features would suggest that, if anything, the new rifle is more reliable than the AKM.

Wooden-stocked AK74s have a horizontal groove running down their stocks, the purpose of which is unknown at the time of this writing, and a muzzle brake similar to that found on tank cannons. Even though the muzzle brake is very effective in reducing recoil, it also creates a large sideward blast (which can be very uncomfortable to those alongside the shooter and can raise dust in prone shooting). It does almost nothing to reduce flash when the weapon is fired at night. To the detriment of left-handed shooters, most AK74s are adjusted to compensate for the sideward movement of the rifle when fired with a right-hand hold; with a left-hand hold, the muzzle brake actually increases the muzzle's sideward movement. This could probably be adjusted by an armorer, however.

Like other versions of the Kalashnikov, the AK74's

gas tube has longitudinal ribs which allow excess gas to blow past the gas piston. Western versions of the rifle like the Valmet and Galil often use a notched gas piston to achieve the same effect. Unlike other Kalashnikovs, the gas tube on the AK74 has a spring washer at its rear to help hold the gas tube in place more securely. The AK74 has a bayonet lug, but bayonets don't appear to be all that common in Afghanistan; as with most modern rifles, this lug is apparently designed more for parade use or guarding prisoners than for actual combat.

The AK74 with side-folding, sheet-metal stock; this stock allows the use of 40-round RPK74 magazines with standard rifles.

The AK74 is only a little lighter than the AKM; this makes it easier to control in full auto fire, but does nothing to decrease the foot soldier's burden nor the amount of raw material needed to produce the rifle. Some saving in material and weight is seen in the ammunition, however, since the M74 is about half as large as the old M43 round.

There are several variants of the AK74. One is the AKS74 which has a plywood, side-folding stock similar to that of the RPKS; another version is made with a side-folding, triangular sheet-metal stock; this change to a side-folding stock may have been made to allow the use of the RPK74's extended 40-round magazines, or possibly because the AKMS folding stock sometimes becomes loose over time.

A short carbine version, known in the West as the AKR Krinkov (or occasionally as the AKSU) is made for use by officers, tank crews, special forces, and the like. This weapon has a greatly abbreviated gas rod and barrel as well as the AKS74's metal folding stock. In order to reduce muzzle blast and make the AKR function reliably, a special muzzle brake has been added to the threaded barrel; a silencer may also be available. The rear sight is mounted on the receiver cover, since the abbreviated barrel of the AKR doesn't allow much room for a rear sight; unlike any other known Kalashnikov variants, the receiver cover of the AKR is hinged to the rear of the barrel.

The AKR Krinkov is made for use by officers, tank crews, special forces, or the like. This weapon has a greatly abbreviated gas rod and barrel as well as the metal folding stock of the AKS74.

While the AKR's muzzle flash and blast are fierce compared to the AK74, it should be remembered that the AKR is the size of a submachine gun but has considerably more power than its pistol-cartridge-firing counterpart. Too, it uses the standard infantry rifle round, simplifying ammunition supply.

A folding-stock light machine gun version, the RPKS74, is also produced by the Soviets. Whether other machine guns or sniper rifles will be created from the AK74 remains to be seen.

Though exact numbers of the various Kalashnikov rifles produced are kept secret, many authorities believe that upward of 15 million AK47 and AKM rifles were produced by the USSR alone, with many millions more produced by other communist countries as well as spin-off designs like the Galil and Valmet. When the Soviets finally rearm their entire army with AK74s, millions more Kalashnikovs will have been added to this figure. Thus, more Kalashnikovs have been manufactured than any other rifle in history; the M1 Carbine and M16 rifle run a distant second and third.

What does the future hold in terms of new Kalashnikov variants? Only time will tell. Improved versions of the AK74 will probably appear in the near future. The likelihood of the Soviets abandoning the basic Kalashnikov design in favor of a totally new one is not too great until some new technology makes the weapon completely obsolete.

One trend in the West is the development of "bullpup" firearms designs. The bullpup design has a lot going for it: it creates a light, short rifle without shortening the barrel to the point where it cuts down on the bullet's velocity or creates excessive muzzle noise and flash. The design places the pistol grip ahead of the magazine and most of the receiver mechanism. The rear of the receiver becomes the butt of the stock. A bullpup-stocked rifle is shorter by nine to ten inches than a regularly stocked rifle with a receiver and barrel of the same length.

The AK47, AKM, and AK74 rifles are ideally suited

for adaptation to the bullpup configuration since their gas rod and recoil spring are located at the front of the receiver, making a stock mechanically unnecessary. This makes it simple to create a bullpup weapon with little modification other than the addition of a higher sighting system and a trigger rod extension system and cover over the receiver. Valmet has already offered a Kalashnikov bullpup version, and while it's doubtful that the Soviets will produce such weapons, other bullpups based on the basic rifle may appear in the near future.

Even though they are very reliable, Kalashnikov rifles and variants aren't noted for accuracy. Part of this has to do with the trigger action, which is generally long and creepy with a sudden let-off. Even given a good trigger pull, accuracy of 6 MOA (minutes of angle) is about the best many AKs can do with standard ammunition; match ammunition will give groups as small as 4 MOA (compared to 0.5-1 MOA by rifles like the U.S. M16A2). Such groups translate to 6- to 4-inch groups at 100 yards—hardly good by Western standards. But this degree of accuracy is adequate for tactics based on firepower and maneuver, with defense of fixed positions carried out by machine guns and other heavy weapons, which is just what the most modern armies use. The Kalashnikovs serve their purpose well.

Western armies may eventually move on to caseless ammunition, multiple-projectile rounds, flechettes, or exotic mechanisms and sighting systems. The Kalashnikov rifles will undoubtedly remain the basis of firearms design for many countries worldwide, given the costs of producing a new type of weapon (and the likelihood that such work might produce only marginal results). Sticking with a proven design and making small improvements in it over time is a safer—and probably wiser—course for the Soviets to follow. The AK74, or some variant, will probably be used into the twenty-first century.

Too, because about 55 countries have adopted some type of Kalashnikov, and because huge numbers of the rifle have been produced and distributed worldwide, "antique" Kalashnikov rifles will probably continue to see use in out-of-the-way places well into the latter part of the twenty-first century and perhaps even into the twenty-second. Kalashnikov rifles will likely dominate the small arms market for at least a century; few other firearms have enjoyed such a long reign.

Specifications for Soviet Rifles

Name	Barrel Length (inches)	Weight (unloaded) (pounds)	Length (inches)	Magazine Capacity
Federov Avtomat	20	9.7	40.9	25
AVS36	24.7	9.8	49.6	15
SVT38	24	8.63	48.1	10
SVT40	24	8.56	48.3	10
SKS45	20.47	8.5	40.2	10 (fixed)
AK47	16.34	9.56	34.25	30
AKM	16.34	7.92	34.25	30
AK74	15.8	7.86	36.6	30
AKR	10 *	6.5 *	26.5 *	30

* Approximate specifications; exact specifications unknown at the time of this writing

Chapter 2

Non-Soviet Variants
of the Kalashnikov Rifle

It is believed that from 36 to over 70 million Kalashnikov rifles have been produced worldwide. These include those made by the Soviet Union, the Eastern Bloc countries, non-aligned countries, China, and North Korea, and Western variant designs made by Israel, South Africa, the Netherlands, Finland, and Egypt.

While some Kalashnikov variants duplicate the original Soviet weapons except for receiver markings, many are distinctly different. The following is a look at the more common non-Soviet Kalashnikov variants.

Bulgaria
Bulgarian-manufactured AK47s and AKMs are identical to their Soviet counterparts right down to the model designations. Most Kalashnikovs used by Bulgaria are manufactured there, although other communist nations have manufactured rifles for Bulgaria in the past; Poland has generally done the lion's share of this work.

China (People's Republic)
China ranks as one of the main manufacturers of

Kalashnikov rifles. Exact numbers are classified, but from 10 to over 20 million of the Chinese Kalashnikovs have probably been made.

Following the communist revolution in China, the new regime inherited a hodgepodge of U.S., Japanese, and Chinese weapons. Because the Soviets were wooing the Chinese during the early 1950s, the USSR supplied the technical know-how to set up small arms factories. Thus, by the mid-1950s, the Chinese had standardized and simplified their ammunition resupply problems by adopting the Soviet Simonov and AK47 rifle.

Chinese weapons designations can be both confusing as well as enlightening. Their "Type" numbers are created by the last two digits of the year in which a firearm is adopted. This gives historians an easy way to figure where the weapon stands in the chronology of things. A problem arises when several small arms are adopted during the same year. For example, the Type 56 *Carbine* is a Simonov SKS45 variation, while the Type 56 *Rifle* is a Kalashnikov design. Things become even more confusing when the Chinese use the term "submachine gun" in sales literature for their Kalashnikov rifles (rather than abiding by the more common idea of submachine guns as stocked weapons using pistol cartridges). Chinese rifle designations can thus be quite confusing to Westerners.

The Chinese Type 56 Rifle is almost identical to the Soviet's third model of the AK47 except for a folding spike bayonet (with a cruciform cross section) which is permanently mounted on the rifle. The Type 56 Rifle has the usual tangent-notch rear sight and is adjustable in gradients from 100 to a fanciful 1,000 meters. A folding stock version, the Type 56-1, is mechanically identical to the standard rifle but usually lacks the bayonet.

Type 56 Rifle barrels are normally chrome-lined to protect the barrel from corrosive ammunition.

Rifles manufactured for export often lack the folding bayonet and are generally marked with "M22" on the receiver or have Roman "L" and "D" markings on the selector (rifles used in China have Chinese characters on their selectors).

As mentioned in Chapter 1, rather than adopt the Soviet AKM, the Chinese designed their own rifle, which looks outwardly like the Soviet SKS, though internally it is actually a modified Kalashnikov design. Fielded in 1968, this is designated the Type 68 Rifle; a few authorities maintain that this actually is the Type 63.

The Type 68 Rifle is selective-fire and has a one-piece wooden stock and the usual folding spike bayonet. Standard AK47/AKM magazines fit the Type 68 if they are modified slightly. The Type 68 Rifle sports an adjustable gas regulator with two settings; it has no known grenade-launching capabilities.

Rumor has it that a Type 73 Rifle (the official designation is unknown) is also being developed. It is believed to be based on the Type 68 design, though outwardly it is said to look more like an AKM since it has a pistol grip and similar sights.

Despite breaking with the Soviet Union, the Chinese have created their own version of the AKM, apparently mostly for export to countries including the United States and Iraq, as well as to rebels in Afghanistan and Nicaragua.

To add to the confusion, the AKM version is still designated as the Type 56 Rifle. Visual inspection quickly shows the difference between the two rifles, however, since the milled steel receiver of the AK47-style rifles has a long milled lightening slot on each side of the receiver over the magazine well while the AKM version has the usual dimple over the well. Unlike most AKM variants, the Chinese rifle has no reinforcement ribs on the receiver cover. As with many other Kalashnikovs, the Type 56 rifle has a cleaning kit stored in a small trapdoor container in the butt of the stock and a cleaning rod mounted under the barrel.

A Chinese semiauto AKM version is still designated as being a Type 56 Rifle even though it has a stamped sheet-metal body rather than one of milled steel. Quick identification can be made by the AKM "dimple" on the receiver's side over the well.

In addition to the folding-stock Type 56-1, the Chinese have developed their own folding-stock model of the AKM, the Type 56-2 Rifle. This rifle's stock is made of sheet metal with a plastic cheekpiece. The stock folds to the right of the receiver, which is a bit awkward since it covers the selector if it is in the "fire" position. These rifles generally have no bayonet and have red-brown furniture (i.e., pistol grip, stock, and fore grip) made of layers of fiberglass soaked in epoxy plastic. At the time of this writing, these three Chinese AKM variants appear to have been modified slightly and adopted as the Type 81 Rifle.

Many of the Chinese rifles are being made without

permanently mounted bayonets; it may be that the Chinese have realized that such weapons aren't often needed in combat when the firepower of an assault rifle is readily available. (Interestingly enough, spike bayonets—as well as Soviet-style bayonets—are finding their way onto many of the newer rifles being exported to the United States.)

Chinese Kalashnikovs imported into the United States are often marketed as AKS rifles (the "S" apparently stands for "semiautomatic"); this produces a bit of confusion, since the Soviet "S" designation normally designates a folding stock. The drum designed for the Chinese Type 81 LMG is also often offered for sale in the United States since it fits the Chinese rifle as well. These export rifles have stocks that are made of tough Chu wood which seems to be quite impervious to abuse; the pistol grips on the import rifles are often modified from the standard Chinese shape to a larger one more like that of the Soviet rifles; many also have a larger safety lever that is easier to manipulate.

In the mid-1980s, the Chinese started producing rifles chambered for the .223 Remington. This led to speculation that they would adopt that round for their military; in fact, these rifles are for export, and the Chinese seem uninterested in switching to a smaller cartridge for the time being. These .223 rifles are imported to the United States in a semiauto version usually designated the AKS-223. Early AKS-223 rifles were far less reliable than other models of the Kalashnikov due to problems with the magazines and too-small gas ports. Current models approach the reliability of the 7.62x39mm Kalashnikovs.

Two different Chinese branches of government presently handle the export of the AK rifles. One is Norinco

(China North Industries Corporation), which is run by a marketing arm of the government which is under the control of the Ministry of Military Armament. The other is PTK (Poly Technologies) International, Inc., which is connected directly to the Ministry of Military Armament. This division must make perfect sense to the Chinese bureaucracy, but it creates confusion for those purchasing rifles from China.

At the time of this writing, three types of stocks are found on AKM-style Chinese semiauto rifles imported into the United States. One is a standard wooden stock (like the Type 56) while the two others are the folding stocks of the Type 56-1 and Type 56-2. The names used in marketing these rifles varies greatly; the Type 56 is often called the AKS-762, and the folders are generally known as Type 56-1 or Type 56-2, with an "S" often being added to denote their semiauto-only design. A milled-receiver, AK47-style semiauto has also been recently marketed in the United States; this is sometimes designated the AK-47/S.

Slightly modified versions of the Type 56, chambered for the .223/5.56mm NATO, are currently coming into the United States from Norinco as the 84S (standard stock, semiauto) and 84S-1 (folding stock version). The most noticeable change on these is the addition of a fairly good flash hider rather than the usual muzzle nut found on most Chinese-made AKs. The model numbers used with guns exported to the United States suggests that model changes were made in 1976 and again in 1984.

The front sights of Chinese Kalashnikovs differ slightly from those of many other communist countries. Rather than having two curved dog ears on either side of the sight post, the entire post is surrounded by a circle of sheet metal. The top of this hoop has a large circular hole cut into it to allow elevation adjustment of the front sight. A number of accessories are also exported by China, including bayonets, magazines, magazine carriers, and drum magazines.

Fleming Firearms modified Chinese AKs to create its Mini-47 with selective-fire capabilities and a twelve-inch barrel. Cyclic rate is reduced to 500 rpm and the modified firearm is quite reliable and similar in concept to the AKR Krinkov.

Modified versions of the Chinese rifles are often encountered. Perhaps the most interesting of these is the Fleming Firearms "Mini-47" modification, which was based on a folding-stock AKS. The rifle is selective-fire, with the barrel shortened to twelve inches (along with shortened gas tube, cleaning rod, and piston). The Mini-47 weighs 7.7 pounds and has an overall length of only 22.6 inches with the stock folded. The cyclic rate is reduced to 500 rpm and the modified firearm is quite reliable and similar in concept to the Soviet AKR Krinkov. An identical modification was made by Fleming to the Valmet M76 rifles.

Czechoslovakia

The Czech Vz58 was introduced in 1958 and is outwardly patterned after the AK47. The rifle is seen in two versions, the Vz58P with standard stock and the Vz58V with metal single-strut folding stock. Early models have wooden furniture, while newer ones have wood fiber/plastic or even all-plastic furniture. These selective-fire rifles are chambered for the 7.62x45mm Czech, which is identical to the Soviet M43 round.

Internally the Vz58 is quite different from its Soviet counterpart. The principal difference is a bolt which tilts to lock in place; the rifle also has a simplified trigger mechanism and a thumb-operated selector (similar to the AR-15 rifle). The receiver cover is designed so that dust will stay out without a cumbersome safety/charging handle slot cover.

Though the Vz58 rifle is only slightly smaller than its Soviet counterpart, it weighs 2-1/2 pounds less empty (it is lighter to carry, but it is also harder to control in automatic fire since it has no muzzle compensator). A bipod, special bayonet, and cone-shaped flash hider are available for the rifle. The bipod attaches below the front sight to the bayonet mount.

East Germany

The East Germans have produced weapons nearly identical to the Soviet AK47 and AKM and are currently working on their own version of the AK74. The German designations make use of the abbreviation for *Maschinenpistole* (machine pistol) followed by the first letter of the inventor's name and any letters or numbers that differentiate it from other weapons. Thus, the AKM becomes the MPiKM—*Maschinenpistole Kalashnikova Modern*—and the folding-stock version of the AKM becomes the MPiKMS.

The first East German Kalashnikov rifles were copies of the third model of the AK47. The MPiK was the wooden-stocked version and the MPiKS was the folding-stock version; the only noticeable difference between these rifles and those of the Soviets was the omission of the cleaning rod under the barrel and the cleaning kit in the stock.

In addition to direct copies of the Soviet AKM and AKMS, East Germany also produced its own side-folding stock AKM which was designated the MPiKMS72. It is believed that East Germany is now producing its own version of the Soviet AK74.

The East German AKMs were direct copies of the Soviet AKM and AKMS; the MPiKM was the wooden-stock version and the MPiKMS was the folding-stock version. The East Germans also produced their own AKM with a side-folding stock, designated the MPiKMS72; the heavy wire stock folds to the right of the receiver.

A small training rifle modeled after the MPiKM has also been made by East Germany; it is designated the KKMPi69 and fires the .22 LR rimfire. It is readily distinguished from the standard rifles because it lacks a gas tube.

Egyptian Misr

The Egyptians purchased large numbers of AK47s from the Soviet Union during the 1950s; by the end of that decade, the Soviets helped set up a plant to produce a copy of their AKM. The plant, known as "Factory 54," is part of the Maadi Military and Civil Industries Company run by the government-owned Military Factories General Organization. The Egyptians produce these AKMs as the Misr for Egyptian military use as well as for export (a semiauto version is sold in the States).

The Egyptian AKM has a laminated wood stock and a checkered plastic pistol grip; there is little to distinguish it from the Soviet rifle other than receiver markings.

Finnish Valmet

Because of pressure from the USSR following World War II, the Allies required Finland to dismantle its arms industry. This ban continued until the late 1950s; at that time, Finland started work on a modified AK47. A government-owned combine, Valmet, was created to do the development and production of the new rifle. (In addition to small arms, Valmet manufactures an array of other items, ranging from ships to street cars.)

Between 1958 and 1960, a number of Kalashnikov-based experimental rifles were created. By 1960, two versions were chosen for field tests by the Finnish army; these were designated the M60 rifles. The two models

Finland's *Ryannakkokivaari Malli* 62 (or M62) with standard stock has a distinctive three-pronged flash suppressor and rear-mounted sights which are better than those of most other AKs. Early versions had a rounded pistol grip like the one shown here.

differed most markedly in their triggers; one had a trigger guard and winter trigger while the other lacked a trigger guard of any sort. (Other differences were in flash hiders, bayonet mounts, etc.)

By 1962 a version of one of the rifles was adopted. Designated the *Ryannakkokivaari Malli 62* (or M62), it is found in two models, the standard-stock M62 and the folding-stock M62T.

One of the most distinctive features of the Valmet rifles, including the M62 and all subsequent variations, is the open-ended, three-pronged flash suppressor with a bayonet lug on its lower side. In addition to flash suppression, the end can quickly cut barbed wire by pushing the muzzle onto a strand of wire and firing a round —noisy but effective.

The Valmet Kalashnikovs have a distinctive, three-pronged flash hider. This effective device has a bayonet lug on its lower side.

Full-scale production of the M62 started in 1965; most of the work was done by Valmet, although the Finnish SAKO plant handled some of the extra capacity which Valmet couldn't handle due to the large numbers of rifles needed by the military. The basic M62 military rifle was modified slightly in 1969 with flip-up luminous dot sights added for nighttime use; these in turn were replaced with tritium night sights in 1972. Other minor changes have included a better-shaped pistol grip and a strengthened stock.

In 1976 the M62-76 was fielded. This stamped-steel-receiver rifle is similar in concept to the Soviet AKM. Three models were created: the wooden-stock M62-76P, the plastic-stock M62-76M, and the M62-76T with a metal tubular stock which folds to the left of the receiver. As on subsequent Valmet rifles, a sheet-metal stamping protects the magazine release from accidental engagement in heavy brush.

The Valmet M76 rifles have a reversible rear sight, which gives the shooter a choice of either a peep hole (for a faster sight picture) or a square notch.

Several variations of the M62-76 are made for export; Valmet designates these the M71 series. The M71 series has the sheet-metal receiver of the M62-76 rifles but slightly different furniture; the firearms are offered in both .223 Remington and 7.62x39mm. Strangely enough, the rear sight position varies on these models; on some, the sight is placed just in front and above the receiver on the barrel, while on others it is mounted at the rear of the receiver cover (which is usually fitted tightly to prevent the zero from drifting). The receiver-cover mounting of the rear sight gives a much better sight picture. A semiauto version of the M71 was developed for U.S. civilian sales; it was designated the M71S.

Like most Kalashnikovs, this Valmet M76, chambered for 7.62x39mm, has rather optimistic ranges calibrated on its rear sight. A novice might conclude this gun is effective to 600 meters.

In 1976 the M76 family of rifles was created for the export market; the firearms are offered in both selective-fire versions (for military buyers) and semiauto only (for civilian sales). The M76 rifles are offered in 5.56mm NATO/.223 Remington, Soviet 7.62x39mm, and .308 Winchester/7.62mm NATO, and are quite similar in layout to the M71 family. A welcome change in the M76 series is the moving of the rear sight to the receiver cover on all models; this reversible rear sight gives the shooter a choice of either a peephole (for a faster sight picture) or a square notch. The M76 rifles also have a reshaped fore-end and pistol grip; these are closer to the conventional Kalashnikov shapes and are readily distinguished from the conical fore-ends and round ribbed pistol grips of the early M62-77 and M71 firearms.

Many Kalashnikovs have excellent night sights. Shown here is the M76 front sight which flips up to give a glowing circle for aiming.

Valmet added a LMG (light machine gun), the M78, to its export offerings in 1978. In 1982, a rather futuristic bullpup design was added to the lineup as the M82, though it now appears to be discontinued. In 1983, a slightly modified version of the M78, the M78/83S, was offered as a sniper rifle (it, too, appears to be discontinued). The principal difference between this weapon and the M78 was its Dragunov-style stock.

The Valmet M75 family of rifles was created for the export market. Shown here are the metal folding-stock version (top), the standard wooden-stock model (center) and the LMG version, the M78 (bottom). [Photo courtesy of Valmet.]

Like the Finnish military rifles, the export models have three styles of stocks. The "T" in an M76 rifle's designation stands for tubular stock; "F," for folding stock; "W," for wood stock; and "P," for plastic stock. A version of each of the following rifles is offered in either .223 or 7.62x39mm: the M82 Bullpup rifle; the M76F, T, W, and P rifles; the M78/83S sniper rifle (with scope mount and plastic stock); and the M78 LMG (more or less the Finnish equivalent of the RPK). The M78 LMG and M78/83S are also offered in .308 Winchester/ 7.62mm NATO chambering.

The M82's bullpup design would appear to be the next stage in the development of the Kalashnikov rifles, but its poor sales would suggest that the demand for such a rifle may not be too great. Too, rumors continue to circulate about bullpups firing rounds prematurely or exploding from barrel obstructions; since the bullpup

Valmet offers an excellent buffer pad which mounts on the rear of the ejection port. This helps keep hot brass out of the face of left-handed shooters and also is a great help to reloaders.

shooter's face is very close to where the action is in such an occurrence, severe injury would likely result. These rumors may have hurt sales. No actual cases of such blowups were discovered while researching this book. The semiauto M82 bullpups seem to have their following in the United States; their design may still prove to be the wave of the future.

The M82 bullpup was created by placing a one-piece plastic stock over a standard M76 rifle with an abbreviated trigger group. A rod inside the stock connects the forward trigger to the rifle's trigger group. The stock is enlarged on the left side for the shooter's cheek and the sights are canted to the left as well. This keeps shooters from using a left-handed hold, since the reciprocating bolt would be dangerous if held in that manner.

The Valmet M82's bullpup design would appear to be the next stage in the development of the Kalashnikov rifles, but poor sales suggest that the need for such a rifle on the world market may not be great.

The 1980s also saw the introduction of the Valmet Hunter, which is a Kalashnikov rifle in hunting garb with a checkered wooden hunting stock and a wooden fore grip which encloses the gas tube and the barrel below it. Although the Hunter still has a bit of a military look to it, it is a rather attractive firearm; the lower-

than-usual barrel makes follow-up shots quicker than
with most hunting rifles. The rifle is available in .243,
.223, and .308 chamberings, making it ideal for many
hunting purposes. Limited-capacity magazines are also
available for use in hunting. Like other Valmet Kalashnikov rifles, the Hunter comes with an optional ejection
buffer for reloaders.

**The Valmet Hunter is a Kalashnikov rifle barely disguised in
hunting garb. This attractive firearm's low barrel also makes
quick follow-up shots possible.**

Though the field stripping of the Hunter is nearly
identical to that of the other Kalashnikov rifles, it is
necessary to first remove the retaining screw at the rear
of the receiver cover.

The choice of three different chamberings and the
excellent finish of the Valmet firearms sets them above
the standard Kalashnikovs. The rifles are every bit as
reliable as other versions of the Kalashnikov and often a
bit more accurate; only the Galil rifles rival them in this
area.

In 1988, the American-based arm of Valmet, Inc.,
was closed. Valmet rifles imported into the United
States are now handled by Stoeger Industries.

Hungarian AKM/AMD

In the 1950s, Hungary started manufacturing a copy
of the AK47 rifle which was nearly identical to the Soviet AK47. In 1963, Hungary introduced its first version
of the AKM; unlike the AK47, this new gun differed
noticeably from the Russian rifle in its outward layout.

Designated the AKM-63, the Hungarian model has a plastic stock (light gray-blue in early models and green-black in later ones), matching plastic pistol grip, and a forward pistol grip (nearly identical to the rear grip but reversed) under the fore grip with a ventilated metal handguard. The new Hungarian Kalashnikovs have no top covers over their gas piston tube. Care has to be taken when firing long strings of shots since the exposed gas tube and metal handguard can become blisteringly hot.

The Hungarian AKM-63 has a plastic stock, matching plastic pistol grip, and a forward pistol grip under the fore grip with a ventilated metal handguard. The Hungarian Kalashnikovs have no top covers over the gas piston tube.

The AMD-65 is a short version of the Hungarian AKM; it has a single strut folding stock. The barrel and gas rod/piston tube have been shortened to give the rifle a handy overall length and a special muzzle brake mounted on the barrel.

In 1965, the Hungarians modified their AKM design slightly to produce a new rifle, the AMD (or AMD-65). This short version of the AKM has a single strut folding stock which folds to the right. The barrel and gas rod/ piston tube have been shortened to give the rifle a handy overall length, and a special muzzle brake is mounted on the barrel. The muzzle blast and flash are rather excessive with the AMD, but it does fill the role of a submachine gun or paratrooper rifle well and fires a potent round.

The Hungarian AMD in grenade-launcher configuration with folding stock, barrel-extension/gas port assembly. Both the stock and fore grip are spring-loaded to absorb some of the extra recoil of grenade launching. Grenade sight is in the folded position.

A grenade-launching, barrel-extension/gas port assembly is sometimes seen on the AMD. The gas port assembly allows shutting off the gas port so that the weapon won't cycle automatically when the grenade is launched. These modified rifles also generally have a stock and fore grip (without a pistol grip) made to absorb some of the extra recoil of grenade launching; the fore grip actually moves backward during firing; a spring mounted inside it moves it back into position following recoil. A special optical grenade sight is available for this rifle which can fire either the PGR antipersonnel grenade or the PGK anti-armor grenade. Interestingly, both grenades seem to be rocket-assisted so that the recoil of their launching is less than might otherwise be the case for their payload and range.

The Hungarian rifles have a magazine-activated

hold-open device which seems to be a welcome improve-
ment to the Kalashnikov design. Unfortunately, the bolt
falls forward when the magazine is removed and im-
pedes magazine removal. Although this feature can be
of help when cleaning or inspecting a rifle, it is far from
ideal in combat since it actually slows down reloading.

Hungary has exported a number of its rifles. These
are often identical to those used by the Hungarian
military, though some are produced with light beech-
wood furniture. These models generally have the basic
AKM look with a wooden cover over the gas tube and
often lack the pistol grip on the fore-end. Several thousand semiauto versions of these models have made their
way into the United States (Kassnar Imports markets
them as the SA M-85); others have been seen in the
hands of the PLO.

Israel

During the 1967 Arab/Israeli conflict, Israel discovered that its infantry rifle, the FN FAL, didn't function
well in desert conditions, and launched a new program
to develop a combat weapon of its own. Much of the initial testing of candidate rifles used seized Soviet-made
AK47s as well as the FN FALs and M16 rifles which
had been sold by the United States to Israel. After the
tests were completed, the decision was made to create a
rifle based on the AK47 design but chambered for the
5.56mm/.223 Remington cartridge.

Frankenstein-like test weapons were cobbled up using Valmet receivers coupled to Stoner 63 rifle parts,
including the magazine, bolt, and barrel, with some
AK47 parts. After making a number of modifications to
the test rifles (including the addition of an FN FAL-type
folding stock), Israel Military Industries (IMI) started

producing the rifle in 1973, known as the Galil, and it was adopted as the standard Israeli infantry rifle.

Several different variants of the Galil are made. The standard rifle is the ARM (assault rifle/light machine gun); it can be used in a dual role as either a standard rifle or, with bipod and carrying handle, as a SAW (squad automatic rifle). The short-barreled SAR (short assault rifle) lacks the bipod mount under its front sight. The standard magazine carries 35 rounds; 50-round magazines are also available but unfortunately are too long for use with the bipod. Although somewhat gimmicky, the bipod can double as a somewhat awkward wire cutter—a feature that might be valuable in combat. A 12-round ballistic magazine for launching grenades is also available.

The M16-style sights on the Galil are placed on the gas cylinder and at the rear of the receiver cover in the same manner used on the Valmet M76 rifles. The rear sight is a copy of the AR-15 flip-type "L" arrangement with one peep sight set for 300 meters and the other for 500. Although somewhat awkward, all windage and elevation adjustments are made on the hooded front sight; a screwdriver is used to adjust windage and a special tool to change elevation. Night sights (behind the front sight and to the front of the rear sight) with tritium glow-in-the-dark markings flip up for use on all models; the Nimrod sniper scope is available for the standard rifle, though it is generally used on the .308 sniper version.

The bayonet lug is mounted on the upper side of the barrel just in front of the front sight. Cutoff valves on the gas port just below the front sight enable the Galil rifle to be used as a grenade launcher with appropriate ballistic cartridge and rifle grenade. The AR-15-style flash suppressor accommodates this use. (This flash hider was used on early Galils imported into the United States; as of 1988, a new muzzle brake similar to that of the FN FAL is to be found on the imported rifles.)

In addition to the standard sheet-metal ejection port cover/selector on the right side, the Galil rifles have a conveniently located thumb selector on the left side of the receiver over the pistol grip. The selector still makes the "Kalashnikov clack" when switched, but it's considerably more convenient for right-handed users than the standard arrangement, and makes it possible to release the safety without removing the hand from the grip.

One unique feature of the Galil design is the projection on the lower side of the handguard; this is a bottle opener (yes, Chevy Chase fans, there *is* a rifle with a built-in bottle opener). Apparently Israeli troops had the bad habit of using M16 and FN FAL magazines for bottle openers and often ruined magazine lips; the designers of the Galil felt that the new rifle's reliability would be helped greatly by adding this feature.

Many Galil rifles are exported and sometimes have a plastic or wooden stock rather than the folding metal stock, with either plastic or standard wooden fore grips. Lettering on the selector/safety of these models is generally in Roman characters rather than the Hebrew characters used on Israeli military rifles.

In the United States, two semiauto models of the ARM are often encountered. These generally have a rounded plastic fore grip rather than the standard square grip. One of these export models is chambered for the standard .223 and the other for .308 Winchester/7.62mm NATO; the .308 rifle has both 5- and 25-round magazines available. An adapter kit was also offered with the Galil when imported into the United

States by Magnum Research. This consisted of a wooden fore grip, carrying handle, and bipod. A scope adapter was also offered for both rifles.

Semiauto model of the Galil ARM with the standard square fore grip and folding stock. This rifle is chambered for the .308 Winchester/7.62mm NATO and has a 25-round magazine. [Photo courtesy of Magnum Research.]

In the late 1980s, Action Arms took over importing the Galil and for a time offered an adapter for using AR-15/M16 magazines in the .223 rifle. This accessory acts as a magazine well extension and is held in place by the magazine release. A second magazine release located on the adapter's left side engages the AR-15 magazines; the magazines are released by pushing on the rear end of this new release. The unit worked well but carried a rather high price tag, which may be why it is no longer offered. At the time of this writing, Action Arms offers a number of other accessories, including a scope adapter and the 50-round magazine for the .223 rifle.

The company markets the .308 and .223 versions of the gun in three configurations. One is the AR (assault rifle) which has a plastic fore grip. Another version is the ARM (assault rifle, military), which is nearly identical to the military rifle with its wooden fore grip; these rifles also have a bipod and carrying handle. A sniper version is also imported into the United States; it is based on the .308 version but has a heavier barrel (see the chapter on sniper rifles for more information).

Galil ARM with plastic fore grip often encountered in the US. This rifle is chambered for .223 Remington. Note excellent safety, sights, and flash hider, often missing from communist versions of the rifle. [Photo courtesy of Magnum Research.]

The Galil has the same reliability of other AKs and a few of the drawbacks, since it still is rather heavy and makes a bit of noise when the safety is operated. Unlike many other Kalashnikovs, it is capable of fairly good accuracy thanks to good sights, has scope mounts readily available, and uses the effective .223 round. This all makes it a strong contender in the Free World's assault rifle contest, and many feel the Galil is the best of the Kalashnikov variations produced to date.

Netherlands
The Netherlands has been licensed to build Galil rifles for its military. Its 5.56mm rifle is designated the MN1.

North Korean Types 58 and 68
The North Korean Type 58 rifle is virtually identical

to the third pattern Soviet AK47; this was made in both the fixed wooden stock and folding-stock versions.

North Korea's Type 68 rifle is its version of the Soviet AKM. It is identical except that the front grip is similar to that of the AK47 rather than the thicker AKM style, and the internal safety device (rate reducer) is missing. Folding-stock versions of the Type 68 are also made; these stocks are quite different in appearance from those of the AKMS in that the two arms have large perforations in them, apparently to reduce the rifle's weight.

North Korea's Type 68 is identical to the Soviet AKM except the front grip is closer to that of the AK47 than the thicker AKM style. Folding-stock versions (as shown here) are also made; these stocks have large perforations in their arms.

North Korea has made considerably more Kalashnikovs than it needs. The surplus has been exported to a number of countries in the Middle East and Africa. These rifles are readily identified by the Korean characters on the selector and other points on the receiver; finish on the wood and metal of the Korean rifles is generally inferior to that of other countries.

Polish kbkAK and kbkAK-DGN

AK47s identical to the Soviet model were made in Poland; these were designated the kbkAK.

A version of the AKM has been manufactured in

Poland since the early 1960s; it is virtually identical to the Soviet rifle except for a flange compensator. This rifle is designated the kbkAK-DGN (also known as the PMK in the West). When this rifle is modified to launch the DGN/60 grenade, it is designated the kbkAK-DGN-60 (or PMK-DGN-60). In this configuration, the rifle has a removable barrel adapter/launcher, a detachable rubber recoil stock boot, a 10-round magazine with a block to prevent anything other than ballistic rounds being loaded into it, special grenade sights, and a gas cutoff switch on the gas tube to allow single shots without cycling (and perhaps damaging) the action.

The Polish kbkAK-DGN-60 (or PMK-DGN-60) has a removable barrel adapter/grenade launcher, a detachable rubber recoil stock boot, a 10-round magazine, special grenade sights, and a gas cutoff switch on the gas tube.

Romanian AIM and AKMS

Romania has manufactured the AIM, based on the Soviet AKM, since the late 1960s. The AIM is basically identical to the Soviet AKM with minor changes, including a laminated wood pistol grip on the lower side of the handguard. These are readily distinguishable from the Hungarian AKD grips; they are curved or rounded rather than similar to the rear grip of the Hungarian grips.

In 1970, Romania fielded a folding-stock version of the AIM, designated the AKMS; in addition to the folding stock, the pistol grip on the fore-end of this weapon doesn't curve forward as on the AIM, and is rounded rather than squared off at the end.

Large numbers of the Romanian rifles are exported to Third World buyers.

The Romanian AIM is identical to the Soviet AKM with a minor change in the addition of a laminated wooden pistol grip/handguard. Large numbers of the Romanian rifles are exported to Third World buyers.

The Romanian folding-stocked AKMS has a pistol grip fore-end which doesn't curve forward (as on the AIM) and is rounded off rather than squared off at the end.

South Africa

Before 1977, the South African state arms agency, ARMSCOR, manufactured the FN FAL as the R1 rifle. With the United Nations arms embargo against South Africa and the problem of well-armed guerrillas with Russian and Chinese weapons, ARMSCOR expanded practically overnight in order to supply South Africa with the weapons it needed.

During the late 1970s, ARMSCOR obtained a license from Israel to manufacture a slightly modified version of the Galil rifle; the South African versions of the Galil are now issue weapons. The ARM version is designated the R4 rifle and the SAR version the R5. The principal change in the South African versions of the rifle are in the carbon fiber-reinforced composite stock, which is cooler in the hot sun. Too, the stock was lengthened slightly to accommodate the larger size of the average Afrikaner. The twist rate of the barrel has been increased very slightly and the overall weight of the rifle is greater. A semiauto version of the rifle, the LM-4, is also produced for civilian use. A second-generation passive night scope, the Kentron Eloptro MNV, is available for use on the R4 and R5 rifles.

Sweden

In the late 1970s, Sweden tested the Galil in 5.56mm/.223 Remington for possible adoption as its military rifle. The Swedish version was designated the FFV-890C and is nearly identical to the Israeli model save for the rounded plastic fore grip which covers the gas tube as well as the barrel and a faster barrel twist adopted under the mistaken notion that this would cause less severe wounds—in fact, it does the very opposite.

Following military trials, Sweden adopted a version of the FN FNC in .223 Remington rather than the Galil rifle.

Vietnam

In addition to Soviet and Chinese weapons which the North Vietnamese received during their wars with the French and the United States, the Vietnamese inherited a huge store of U.S.-made weapons when the government of South Vietnam fell. This hodgepodge inventory of weapons has made it more or less unnecessary for the Vietnamese to manufacture an infantry rifle of their own to date. However, it seems likely that the Vietnamese will produce a rifle in the near future and that this will be a version of the Soviet AKM, though it is possible that they might leapfrog ahead and produce a copy of the AK74 or the like.

Yugoslavian FAZ

Yugoslavia has produced a number of Kalashnikov variations which are currently part of the FAZ weapons family. These rifles are made at the arms factory of Zavodi Crvena Zastava; while many are created for use by the Yugoslavian army, the country also exports the rifles to many countries, including semiauto versions for the U.S. market, which are imported principally by Mitchell Arms. Fit and finish on the Yugoslavian guns are quite good compared to most communist-made versions of the Kalashnikov and a number of variations have been created for export.

The Yugoslav rifles have a much-needed bolt hold-open arrangement. Because this requires a special cutout in the magazine to work, Soviet magazines won't operate the bolt hold-open unless they are altered.

The Model 64 rifles are based on the third version of the AK47 and have milled receivers. The Model 64 has a standard flash hider, shorter barrel, and 30-round magazine; this version cannot be used to launch grenades. The Model 64A has a grenade-launching attachment on its barrel and a grenade-launcher sight attached to the gas tube. It is generally issued with a 20-round magazine. The 64B is like the 64A, but has a folding steel stock.

Several types of grenades are produced for the rifles, including the M60 antitank, M60 fragmentation, M62 illumination, M62 smoke, and two practice grenades, the M68 (antitank) and M66 (fragmentation).

The Model 70 series has also been created by Yugoslavia. Early Model 70s have the Model 64 milled steel receiver; later rifles use an AKM-style riveted sheet-metal receiver. The M70 is a slightly improved version of the M64; the 70A is the folding-stock version. The Models 70 and 70A have slightly different components and longer barrels and lack finger serrations on their pistol grips, unlike the M64. The M70B1 is a copy of the Soviet AKM and the folding-stock M70AB2, of the AKMS.

The M80 series of rifles are modeled after the Soviet AKM but chambered for the 5.56mm NATO/.223 Remington round. Although these are aimed at the export market, the M80s will probably serve as the basis of a new series of military firearms if Yugoslavia switches to the Soviet M74 round.

Although many Yugoslavian Kalashnikov variations won't accept a bayonet, the country does still make them. Like the Soviet bayonet, the Yugoslavian model doubles as a wire cutter when used with its scabbard; the handle and scabbard are insulated in case the wire being cut is electrified.

Specifications for Non-Soviet Kalashnikov Rifles

Name	Barrel Length (inches)	Weight (unloaded) (pounds)	Length (inches)	Magazine Capacity
Bulgarian AK47	16.34	9.56	34.25	30
Bulgarian AKM	16.34	7.92	34.25	30
Chinese Type 56 (Milled AK47 style)	16.34	9.56	34.25	30
Chinese Type 56 (AKM-style)	16.34	7.92	34.25	30
Chinese Type 68	20.5	7.8	40.5	15
Chinese AKS	16.34	8.2	34.6	30
Chinese AKS-223	17	8.5	34.8	30
Czechoslovakian Vz58	15.8	6.9	33.2	30
E. German MPiK (MPiKS)	16.34	9.56	34.25	30
E. German MPiKM	16.34	7.92	34.25	30
Egyptian Misr	16.34	7.7	34.6	30
Finnish M62	16.5	10.2	36	30
Finnish M76 (.223)	16.75	8	37	15 or 30
Finnish M76 (7.62x39mm)	16.75	8	37	30
Finnish M76 (.308)	20.5	8.25	40.5	20
Finnish M82	17	7.5	27	30
Finnish "Hunter"	20.5	8.2	42	5, 9, 15, and 20
Hungarian AKM	16.34	8	34.3	30
Hungarian AMD	12.6	7.9	30.5	30

Name	Barrel Length (inches)	Weight (unloaded) (pounds)	Length (inches)	Magazine Capacity
Israeli Galil ARM	18.1	8.6	38.6	35 or 50
Israeli Galil SAR	13	7.7	32.3	35 or 50
Israeli Galil (.308) (export model)	21	8.7	41.3	5, 20, or 25
Netherlands MN1	18.1	8.6	38.6	35 or 50
North Korean Type 58	16.34	9.56	34.25	30
North Korean Type 68	16.34	7.82	34.25	30
Polish kbkAK	16.34	9.56	34.25	30
Polish kbkAK-DGN-60	16.34	7.92	34.25	30
Romanian AIM	16.34	7.95	34.25	30
South African R4	18.1	11.7	39.2	35
South African R5	13	9.5	33.3	35
Yugoslavian M64	19.7	8.6	40.9	20
Yugoslavian M64A/ 64B	14.7	8.3	35.9	30
Yugoslavian M70 (70A)	16.3	8.3	37.7	30
Yugoslavian M80	18.11	7.87	38.97	20 or 30

Chapter 3

◎ ─────────────────────────── ◎

Kalashnikov Sniper Rifles

Many military sniper weapons are designed around the various types of assault rifles currently in use by a country's army. This often works well since many modern assault rifles have sufficient accuracy to be used as sniper rifles through the simple expedient of adding a good scope, bipod, and cheek rest. This practice seems to come and go in the West (the German G3; Swiss SG510; various countries' FN LAR; and the U.S. AR-15, M1 Garand, and M14 rifles have all been used as sniper rifles at one time or another), in communist countries, and Western countries which have adopted the Kalashnikov action.

Given that the Kalashnikov rifle's strong suit is not accuracy, it may seem a strange weapon on which to base a sniper rifle. But by tuning the weapon with tighter-fitting parts and select barrels, accuracy becomes adequate for most sniper work.

As one can imagine, there are advantages to using a sniper rifle based on the standard-issue rifle. Foremost among these is the short research and development time and low costs involved, since most military rifles are already well debugged and perfected after several years of heavy use. Military supply problems are also minimized, since many parts are interchangeable or are similar enough to the standard rifle to allow easy repair by military armorers. Supply of ammunition is also simplified, and even if snipers normally use special-purpose ammunition for accuracy, they can usually fall back on standard-issue cartridges should they run low.

On the individual level, the use of a self-loading sniper rifle has many advantages for the soldier. Since the sniper rifle operation is nearly identical to standard-issue rifles, the sniper will not spend much time learning how to operate his firearm; rather, he can concentrate on getting the most accuracy from it. Should the sniper be called upon to offer suppressive fire or defend himself at close ranges, the superior firepower of the weapon over a bolt-action sniper rifle is readily apparent. Likewise, the self-loading rifle gives the sniper the ability to make quick follow-up shots or even engage several targets at a time, or to damage planes or similar large equipment with fast-paced multiple shots.

A semiauto rifle also absorbs recoil, making the sniper's work easier. When engaging a single target, it would seem that a bolt-action sniper rifle would be as effective as a semiauto rifle, but in fact the semiauto sniper rifle can give a sniper an edge, since it tames the rifle's recoil. This makes it possible to watch the target through the scope to see if the shot scored a hit or missed. The sniper will also have his rifle ready for a quick second shot if needed without having to manually cycle the weapon. Although snipers aren't supposed to miss the first shot, having a quick second shot ready can be an important plus; many snipers are spotted when operating a bolt action. The Israelis have done some work toward training snipers to engage helicopters as well as destroy fixed wing aircraft on the ground. For such work, they have found a semiauto or even automatic sniper rifle essential to create enough damage to disable the aircraft.

Of course, adapting a military action to sniper use does have its drawbacks. One major problem with the AK rifles (as well as the FN LAR, AR-15, and others) is that the barrel can flex when pressure is placed on it by a bipod or sling. Most bolt-action rifles and a few older-style semiautos employ a one-piece stock and fore grip, but the AK's barrel is supported by the receiver (rather than the stock). Thus, sideward pressure on the Kalashnikov's barrel can cause the point of impact to wander slightly. The change in point of impact by several inches at 100 yards may make little difference to the ordinary infantry soldier, but it matters a great deal to the sniper.

The solution to the problem of barrel flex for most Kalashnikov-based sniper rifles is simply to beef up the receiver and increase the barrel diameter. This does away with the problem but also increases the sniper rifle's weight. However, since much the same solution is used for most bolt-action sniper rifles, the trade-off may not be too great, considering the advantages of a semiauto action.

Methods of minimizing weight without degrading accuracy are available, though they require greater expense or major design changes. Among these are the use of a fluted barrel which keeps the rifle light while maintaining barrel rigidity and the use of a one-piece stock or a foreguard attached to the receiver which allows the barrel to be "free floated" without having pressure placed against it. Placing bipods and slings on the front of the receiver rather than the end of the barrel also helps minimize barrel flex.

Most communist countries use a variation of the Dragunov design. The Soviet Dragunov rifle is chambered for the M1891 7.62x56mmR cartridge; many of the spinoffs used by other countries are chambered for more modern rounds. In the near future, Soviet Dragunovs may be chambered for other rounds commonly used by the Russian army, such as the M74.

Many communist countries have poor quality-control practices. This is especially evident when it comes to manufacturing ammunition. Because of this and the inferior potential accuracy of the Kalashnikov, Soviet snipers and those of many other communist nations are generally incapable of the 0.5 to 1 MOA accuracy normally required of Western snipers. As in other areas of military planning, however, communist countries have tried to make up for this by increasing the number of snipers they deploy.

Militaries in the West seem to be constantly looking for a sniper rifle which offers the ultimate in accuracy, while communist countries have simply created sniper rifles from existing systems and then trained large numbers of men to use them. As with other areas of communist military planning and supply, this has proven to be a less expensive and quicker route than trying to develop a totally new weapon for sniper use. The communist route could also prove superior on the battlefield.

Chinese Type 79

In the late 1970s, the People's Republic of China adopted the Dragunov design as the basis of its Type 79 sniper rifle; the two rifles are virtually identical down to the use of the antiquated 7.62x54mmR cartridge. The Chinese rifle is exported by Poly Technologies, Inc., as the PDM-86 rifle and has been imported by a number of companies, including Navy Arms Company and Keng's Firearms Specialty, Inc.

The Type 79 is a fair sniper rifle, but only passable compared to Western designs which are capable of greater accuracy and chambered for more modern cartridges.

Dragunov

The Soviet *Samozariyadnaya snaiperskaya Vintovka Dragunova* (Self-loading Rifle, Dragunov) was created to replace the M1891/30 Mosin-Nagant bolt-action sniper rifle. Yevgeniy Feodorovich Dragunov is credited with developing the rifle in the late 1950s; it appears that he did his design work under Kalashnikov's direction at the Izhevsk Mashinostroitel'ny Zavod. The Dragunov sniper rifle was adopted by the Soviet army in 1963.

The Soviet Dragunov was created to replace the M1891/30 Mosin-Nagant bolt-action sniper rifle. While Y. F. Dragunov is credited with developing the rifle, it seems probable that he did his design work under Kalashnikov's direction.

The Dragunov differs only in a few minor points from the standard Kalashnikov, the main difference being the M1891 7.62x56mmR cartridge it uses. Apparently the decision to use an antiquated rimmed cartridge was made in order to use existing stocks of the shells; although a rimmed shell is a poor choice for a semiauto design, the Dragunov functions well, partially because of a short magazine. The Kalashnikov trigger design was simplified, since the sniper rifle fires only in a semiauto mode; this change improved the trigger pull. The sniper rifle also uses a short-stroke gas piston to minimize the change in the rifle's balance during recoil and (in theory at least) allows greater accuracy if a follow-up shot is called for.

The receiver has been strengthened for the more powerful cartridge, and the wooden stock has a skeletonized design which creates a pistol grip. The cheek rest is adjustable, but there is no length of pull or other butt adjustment common on Western sniper rifles. The barrel has iron sights similar to those of the standard Kalashnikov and ends with a fluted "bird cage" flash hider similar to that of the M16.

The barrel is neither overly heavy nor fluted, so that the Dragunov lacks some of the accuracy normally expected from a sniper rifle. Groups from an average Dragunov would probably be in the 1.5 to 2 MOA range at best; some authorities feel it is probably much worse given the poor quality of some Soviet ammunition. Even so, for torso shots within ranges of several hundred yards, the Dragunov would have the accuracy needed to do its job.

The Dragunov's scope mount fastens onto the left side of the receiver. Scopes used on the Dragunov include the PS01 (currently in use) as well as the PU, PE, and SVT40 series. Interestingly, the 4x PS01 can detect active infrared night-vision equipment through the use of an internal filter. This filter can also act like a night-vision scope if a bright infrared source is available, but such use is marginal at best.

The scope's viewing field is graduated in one corner

so that the sniper can estimate the range to his target by bracketing a standing man. Ranging brackets are in 100-meter increments and go beyond 1,000 meters (pretty optimistic, given the accuracy potential of the rifle). In order to extend the hours at which the sniper can operate, a small battery-operated electric bulb illuminates the scope's reticles in dim light.

Like other versions of the Kalashnikov, the Dragunov takes advantage of proven technology to create a rifle that is easy to produce and maintain. This, in turn, allows the Soviet Union to produce and field larger numbers of weapons than would otherwise be the case. The Soviets place great importance on the deployment of the sniper (a lesson learned from the Germans in World War II); the Dragunov allows them to create the number of snipers called for.

The Medved ("Bear") is the Soviet sporter version of the Dragunov. This rifle looks quite different since it has an integral magazine, different receiver cover, and a sport-style wooden stock.

The Soviet Union also produces a sporter version of the Dragunov. This rifle looks quite different since it has an integral magazine, a different receiver cover, a sporter-style wooden stock, and a simplified scope. The rifle is known as the *Medved* (Bear).

Galil Sniper Rifle

While the Israelis had used accurized M14 rifles for sniping purposes for some time, following their switch to the Galil rifle, work was done to create a Kalashnikov-based sniper rifle. The result was a heavy-barreled Galil rifle chambered for the .308 with a special muzzle brake normally mounted, although Israeli snipers apparently often use silencers as well. When in place, the silencer counters recoil, keeps from stirring up dust from the muzzle blast, and hides the position of the sniper somewhat, although the supersonic bullet crack will still result unless subsonic ammunition is used.

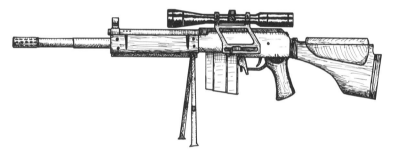

The Galil sniper rifle has a heavy barrel with an FN FAL-style muzzle brake. The bipod is mounted in front of the receiver and its legs fold forward under the fore grip when not in use.

Because of the Kalashnikov's tendency to shift its point of impact when a bipod is placed on the end of its barrel, the Israelis have mounted the bipod just in front of the receiver. When not in use, the bipod's legs fold forward under the fore grip. The wooden stock can be folded for compact storage. The stock has an adjustable comb and a heavy rubber butt plate.

The Israeli-made Nimrod ranging scope is normally mounted on the Galil sniper rifle. The scope is offset to the left of the receiver, making left-handed shooting nearly impossible. Iron sights are kept on the rifle for emergency or close-range use. The Galil sniper is the most accurate of the Kalashnikov-based sniper rifle designs.

Limited numbers of the Galil sniper rifle have been imported into the United States by Action Arms for possible use by police snipers.

Polish SVD

The Polish SVD is a direct copy of the Soviet Dragunov. Quality is of the same standard as the Soviet weapon.

Romanian FPK

Romanian AKM rifles are designed so that the bolt carrier travels farther than is necessary for the 7.62x39mm round. This allowed Romanian designers to create a sniper rifle around the basic AKM rifle that chambers a longer cartridge.

The Romanian sniper rifle was fielded in 1980 and is chambered for the 7.62x54mmR cartridge. The basic changes from the standard Kalashnikov are in two receiver-strengthening plates and a new barrel with a special muzzle brake.

In 1980, this change was taken advantage of to create a 7.62x54mmR sniper rifle. The basic changes consisted of beefing up the receiver with two strengthening plates and placing a new barrel with a special muzzle brake on the rifle's receiver. Other changes included reworking the bolt face, lengthening the gas piston, adding a new laminated wooden skeleton stock, and creating a new shortened magazine.

The Romanian rifle might be adapted to other

cartridges, including the 7.62mm NATO; other chamberings might be created for export.

Valmet M78/83S

During the early 1980s, Valmet modified its long-barreled, bipod-equipped M78 by adding a modified stock and scope mount to create the M78/83S sniper rifle.

The Valmet M78/83S is a modified version of the Finnish SAW. Chambered for .308 Winchester/7.62mmNATO, the rifle has Valmet's excellent prong-style flash hider and iron sights with glow-in-the-dark inserts for emergency use at night.

The M78/83S is made in .308 Winchester/7.62mm NATO chambering. Valmet offers scope mounts along with the M76 scope-mount adapter which fits on both the M78 and M78/83S rifles. The M78 and M78/83S barrels both have excellent prong-style flash hiders which minimize flash in low-light conditions; the iron sights have glow-in-the-dark inserts for emergency use at night.

Externally and internally, overall fit and finish of the Valmet rifles is much better than that of most communist sniper rifles. The rifles are a bit more accurate as well, with only the Galil snipers boasting better accuracy.

Yugoslavian M76

The Yugoslavians have created a sniper rifle from their M70B1 rifle. Early models of the M76 sniper rifle have milled steel receivers like that of the third model AK47; current M76 sniper rifles are based on the AKM-style receiver.

The principal change made to create the sniper rifle was to chamber it for the 7.92x57mm Mauser round (rather than the 7.62 NATO of the M70B1). The Mauser round was the cartridge used for the previous Yugoslavian bolt-action sniper rifle as well as their machine guns; machinery to produce the cartridges was already in place and ready to use.

Like other Yugoslavian AKs, the teakwood furniture on the M76 is modified with a fuller pistol grip. The stock also has a different cut and sports a heavy rubber butt pad to help deal with increased recoil. The barrel itself is considerably longer than that of the standard rifle and has a flash hider similar to the Dragunov's. Although the trigger pull of the M76 is long and creepy, pull is generally in the 3.25- to 4-pound range, making it fairly good for sniping.

The M76 is normally issued with a 4x scope designated the PSO-1. The scope is patterned after the Soviet PSO-1 used on the Dragunov but has a tritium illumination element rather than a battery and electric light. A passive night-vision scope, the PN5X80(j) is also available for the M76; the scope has 5x power and uses rechargeable batteries.

As with other Kalashnikov rifles, the M76's potential accuracy is not all one might hope for but generally sufficient for the tasks required of it.

Yugoslavian M77B1

These rifles are based on the FAZ rifles which were created to fill the RPK's LMG role. As such, they are generally identical to the M77B1 with the main addition being a scope (see next chapter for more information on the M77B1). These rifles are available in .223 Remington, 7.62x39mm, and .308 Winchester; the latter is most suited to sniper use. With the addition of a scope, these rifles make fair sniper rifles, but their accuracy does not seem to be nearly as good as most Western weapons. Semiauto, heavy barrel versions of these rifles are currently imported into the United States by Mitchell Arms.

Specifications for AK Sniper Rifles

Name	Barrel Length (inches)	Weight (unloaded) (pounds)	Length (inches)	Magazine Capacity
Chinese Type 79	24.5	9.46	48.2	10
Dragunov	24	9.5	48.2	10
Galil (.308)	21	17.6	43.8	20
Polish SVD	24	9.5	48.2	10
Romanian FPK	21	10.69	45.5	10
Valmet M78/83S	24.25	11	43.5	20
Yugoslavian M76	21.8	11.6	45.4	10
Yugoslavian M77B1	19.6	11.4	40.6	30

Chapter 4

Semiautomatic Weapons and Light Machine Guns

The design team (OKB) Kalashnikov assembled at the Izhevsk Mashinostroitel'ny Zavod has created several heavier Kalashnikov-based weapons. These became the basis of the Soviet LMGs (light machine guns) and GPMGs (general-purpose machine guns).

As in the West, there is some confusion as to what role the carrier of the LMG plays at the squad level since all the members of the group carry weapons that can be used in automatic mode. Nevertheless, both the East and West are intent on producing such weapons; the United States uses the Minimi; England, the LSW; Italy, the Beretta 70/78; Austria, an AUG with a heavy barrel. All are chambered in the standard infantry rifle round. Likewise, the Soviet Union and most communist countries have adopted the RPK, which is basically a heavy-barrel version of their assault rifle. Exactly where this trend will lead remains to be seen.

In the interest of simplifying research and development efforts and troop training, many countries also produce MMGs (medium machine guns) based on standard infantry rifles. Examples of these are the Heckler

& Koch series of rifles/machine guns, the Stoner 63 weapons, and the Soviet PK. Interestingly, while the West prides itself on producing easy-to-use equipment, advanced training, and teaching concepts, it has lagged far behind the communist countries in fielding families of weapons which can all be operated in the same manner with a minimum of training.

As with the AK47, AKM, and AK74 rifles, several other countries have adopted the basic Soviet machine gun designs to their own use as well.

Chinese Type 81 LMG

The Chinese Type 81 LMG is a direct copy of the Soviet RPK, although the 75-round drum the Chinese use is a bit different from the original.

A semiauto version of the weapon, designated the RPKS-75, was imported and sold in the United States for some time by the Navy Arms Company and Keng's Firearms Specialties. The "S" in its designation denotes its semiauto-only capabilities rather than a Soviet-style folding stock. Offered in both 7.62x39mm as well as .223 Remington, this version of the Kalashnikov uses a standard AK47 rear sight with increments from 100 to 800 meters (rather than up to 1,000 as on the Soviet RPK), which is still a bit optimistic for the abilities of either round. The barrel is lighter than that of the RPK, and a different muzzle brake, similar to a Cutts compensator and found on the Type-81 LMG as well, is mounted on its end.

East German LMG-K

The East German LMG-K is a direct copy of the Soviet RPK. As the East Germans switch to the M74 round, a new machine gun chambered for the M74 and similar to the Soviet RPK74 will probably be fielded.

Finnish M78

The M78 or AVM78 (*Automaattikivaari Valmet Malli* 1978) is a heavy-barrel version of the M76 rifle developed by Valmet which, in turn, is based on the Kalashnikov and bears the same relationship to the Finnish infantry rifle as the Soviet RPK does to the AKM.

The Finnish M78 or AVM78 (top) is a heavy-barrel version of the Valmet M76 (bottom).

Like most other PK-style SAWs, the Finnish M78 has a heavy barrel which cannot be changed in the field. The rifle has a bipod and a spring-loaded carrying handle which lies across the receiver when not in use.

Like the RPK, the weapon has a heavy barrel which cannot be changed in the field. The rifle also has a bipod and an excellent spring-loaded carrying handle which retracts out of the way to the side of the receiver when not in use. These rifles are exported by Valmet in both semi-auto and selective-fire versions in 5.56mm NATO, 7.62x39mm, or 7.62mm NATO chamberings. A slightly modified version is also offered as a sniper rifle. In addition to the standard M76 box magazine, a 75-round drum magazine is made for the M78.

Israeli Galil ARM

This rifle is the standard-issue Galil infantry rifle which is made to serve as an SAW with the addition of a bipod and carrying handle. As an SAW, the rifle is not without problems. Because its barrel is no heavier than that of the issue rifle, it is as prone to overheating. Too, the 50-round magazine hangs up if used for prone shooting; a drum magazine or the like isn't available so that the rifleman using the rifle as an LMG actually may have less firepower than others in the squad who can use the longer magazines.

It seems likely that the Israelis will issue a heavy-barrel version of this rifle, possibly with a drum magazine, in the near future. Until then, it is more or less a weapon which offers few capabilities which the standard-issue rifle does not.

Romanian RPK

Chambered for the M43 7.62x39mm cartridge, this rifle is nearly identical to the Soviet RPK except for the bipod, whose legs can be extended independently to different lengths.

Romanian PK

The Romanian PK machine guns are virtually identical to the Soviet PK. The PK, PKB, PKS, and PKT versions are all represented in the Romanian military. About the only difference between the Romanian PK and the Soviet machine gun is a slightly different bipod.

Soviet RPK

The RPK *(Ruchnoi Pulemet Kalashnikova*—Kalashnikov's Light Machine Gun), introduced in 1961, is basically a strengthened AKM with a longer and heavier barrel. Interestingly enough, the RPD *(Ruchnoi Pulemet Degtyaryov),* which the RPK replaced, was a modified machine gun design which had been made to look like the Kalashnikov when it was first fielded in 1953, even though it was considerably different internally. The Chinese and Koreans also produced copies of the RPD, designated by the Chinese as the PRC Type 56 and Type 56-1 light machine guns, and the Type 62 by the Koreans.

The RPD was belt-fed with the round box lying below the receiver; the basic mechanism which lifted the belt of ammunition to the receiver had very little power and often failed when the firearm's mechanism became dirty. It is little wonder the firearm was replaced by the RPK; the amazing part of the story is that the RPD was ever fielded at all.

The RPK fires the 7.62x39mm cartridge and accepts the standard AKM magazine as well as the 40-round box and 75-round drum magazines designed for it. One drawback to the RPK is that it does not have a quick-change barrel and fires from a closed bolt. Thus, by Western standards, it would seem to be prone to overheating and accuracy would undoubtedly suffer with extended use. Lack of a quick-change barrel forces the gunner to fire short bursts with not more than 80 to 90 shots fired per minute during periods of heavy fire or face the possibility of having his weapon trashed by overheating.

In addition to lacking a quick-change barrel, the rifle also has no way to regulate the amount of gas cycling the action. This undoubtedly causes extra wear and tear when the RPK is clean and makes it prone to poor functioning when used excessively without cleaning.

The RPK is equipped with a folding bipod similar to that used on the RPD; the stock has a downward curve to allow the off hand to hold the firearm to the shooter's shoulder. The bipod is fairly high in order to avoid getting hung up on the 40-round magazine; a heavy spring between the legs of the bipod allows it to be deployed quickly.

The rear sight of the RPK has windage markings and is adjustable in elevation in 100-meter increments to 1,000 meters. Some RPKs have a bracket designed to accept scopes or night-vision equipment. As with the AKM, the RPK has a luminous dot on its rear sight.

Some time after the RPK was introduced, a folding stock model was also fielded. This weapon is designated the RPKS; the wooden stock folds onto the left side of the receiver.

Soviet RPK74

As might be expected, the creation of the AK74 led to a weapon similar to the RPK chambered for the new, smaller M74 round. The RPK74 is nearly identical to the AK74 save for a longer, heavier barrel, slightly different stock, and the rear sights and bipod of the original RPK. A folding-stock version of the gun is designated the RPKS74; it uses the folding stock mechanism of the AKS74.

Like the RPK, the RPK74 lacks a quick-change barrel and fires from a closed bolt; nevertheless, it seems to fill the role the Soviets see for it.

The Soviet RPK74 is nearly identical to the AK74 rifle but has a longer, heavier barrel, slightly different stock, and the rear sight and bipod of the original RPK.

Soviet PK/PKM

The Kalashnikov design teams also created the PK *(Pulemet Kalashnikova)* which served as the Soviet MMG. The PK machine guns fire the old Mosin-Nagant 7.62x54mmR rimmed cartridge; the PK's receiver is strong enough to handle its power and uses a belt-feed system which overcomes problems created by the rimmed cartridge in box magazines. In order to accommodate the belt-feed mechanism, the PK models have inverted gas piston/barrel positions and an upside-down bolt. Much the same technique was used by Fabrique Nationale in its MAG design and by Stoner on his 63 Systems machine guns.

The gas piston powers the feed pawls of the weapon; the rimmed rounds have to be stripped from the belt before they can be chambered (this system seems to be patterned after the Czech M52 machine gun). The trigger group appears to be adapted from the Soviet RPD.

The PK weapons usually have a laminated wooden stock with a cutout which facilitates easier control of the weapon during firing; a sling is normally threaded through this hole. A cleaning brush is stored in this stock.

The PK *(Pulemet Kalashnikova)* serves as the Soviet MMG. The PK machine guns fire the very effective 7.62x54mmR cartridge; the receiver of the PK is strong enough to handle its power and the cartridges are fed into the weapon on a belt.

When the weapon is mounted on a bipod, the box holding the belted ammunition is fastened beneath the receiver to keep the machine gun balanced. When the PK is mounted on a tripod, the ammunition box is generally mounted to the left and under the receiver; the belted rounds feed into the right side of the receiver.

PKs have quick-change fluted barrels so that they can be replaced with a spare when heavy firing causes them to overheat; a large carrying handle mounted on the barrel aids in its removal. Flash hiders similar to those of the M16 are mounted on the machine gun's barrel.

The PK's safety is not like that of other Kalashnikov actions; it is located on the left side of the receiver where it can be reached by the thumb. The safe position is to the rear and the fire position is forward. The PK fires in the automatic mode only; skilled users can fire one or two shots at a time by quickly releasing the trigger of the weapon.

An adjustable sleeve gas regulator is found on the gas tube just in front of the bipod. It has three positions: "1" for a clean firearm, "2" for a slightly dirty one, and "3" for a very fouled weapon, poor ammunition, or inclement weather. Adjustments are made using a cartridge rim (perhaps the only justification for using rimmed cartridges for a modern machine gun design). This regulator undoubtedly helps prevent undue wear when properly adjusted.

A number of versions of the PK have been produced, including a heavy-barreled PKS infantry version on a tripod ("S" stands for *stankovyi,* or "mounted"); a PKB version with spade grips for armored personnel carriers; and the stockless PKT coaxial tank model with an electronic solenoid remote firing control and a conical sheet-metal flash hider.

The stockless PKT version of the PK is designed as a coaxial tank machine gun. The weapon's internal trigger is remote controlled with an electronic solenoid. Unlike other versions of the gun, most PKTs have a conical, sheet-metal flash hider.

A newer "product improved" version of the PK has also been fielded, designated the PKM *(Pulemyot Kalashnikova Modernizirovanniy).* The PKM machine gun has a shoulder rest on its stock and all stamped-steel parts in its feed mechanism. Currently all the models in the PK series are made in the PKM version, whose family consists of the PKM, the tripod-mounted PKMS, and the spade-gripped PKB. The PKB is used on the BRDM, BTR50, and BTR60 armored personnel carriers.

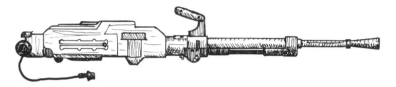

The PKB version of the Soviet PK MMG is designed for use with armored personnel carriers or helicopters. The weapon is stockless and has spade grips with a butterfly thumb trigger.

The Soviet PKS version of the PK has a heavy barrel and is mounted on a tripod (the S in the weapon's designation stands for *Stankovyi,* or mounted).

Soviet 12.7x10.8mm HMG

As one might expect, the Kalashnikov action has been adapted by the Soviets to the 12.7x10.8mm Patron, a round more or less the equivalent to the .50 Browning Machine Gun cartridge. The designation for the new HMG (heavy machine gun) is unknown at the time of this writing. It will probably replace the DShK *(Degtyaryova, Shpagina Krupnokalibernyi)* series of machine guns over the next few years.

At the time of this writing, the new large-caliber machine gun has only been seen mounted on new Soviet battle tanks in a configuration similar to that of the Soviet PKT HMG.

Vietnamese TUL-1

The Vietnamese have produced an LMG by placing a new stock, heavy barrel, and bipod on selected Soviet and Chinese AK47 rifles. While the weapon will accept the standard Kalashnikov magazine, these weapons are generally used with a special 75-round drum which appears to be made in Vietnam, though it may be of Russian or Chinese origin.

Yugoslavian M65A and M65B

These rifles are chambered for the 7.62x39mm M43 round and are similar to the RPK in concept, but the M65B has a quick-change barrel, making it better for the role of LMG. Both the M65A and M65B are part of the FAZ group of weapons (variations of the M64 series); both have bipods, distinctive finned barrels (from the gas port back), FN LAR-style carrying handles, and conical flash hiders.

Yugoslavian M72/M77

Based on the Yugoslavian M70 series of rifles, the M72 *(Mitrajez* 1972) is the Yugoslavian version of the Soviet RPK with a heavy barrel and bipod mounted on the standard rifle's receiver. Unlike the RPK, the M72 has a quick-change barrel; the M72B1 has a fixed barrel. Both versions are chambered for the standard 7.62x39mm round and often have a 75-round drum. A gas regulating sleeve is also found on the gas port which, when used properly, would help extend the useful life of the firearm and allow it to be used with a wider range of ammunition than would otherwise be the case.

The M72AB1 is similar to the others in the M72 group but is based on the M70AB1 rifle (a copy of the AKMS); as such, it has a folding stock and a fixed barrel.

Yugoslavia also produces a version of the M77B1 chambered for the 7x39mm, 7.62mm NATO, and .223; this firearm is apparently aimed at the export market; both semiauto-only and selective-fire versions are made. A semiauto version of the M72B1 is currently imported by Mitchell Arms, Inc., as well as several other companies and marketed as the RPK-47 (despite the fact that it has an AKM-style stamped steel receiver rather than the milled AK47-style receiver) or Heavy Barrel RPK. These rifles are readily identified by their fat pistol grip and cooling fins on the barrel from the gas port back.

Furniture on the RPK-47 imported into the United States is generally made of teakwood. Sights are in 100-meter increments from 100 to 1,000 meters. Tritium night sights are also found on these firearms, as is an integral scope mount rail which requires special scope rings available from Mitchell Arms, Inc.

Should Yugoslavia switch to the new Soviet M74 round, a new version of the M80 rifle, chambered for the smaller round, will likely be introduced with the year of introduction determining the model number.

Yugoslavian M80

The M80 *(Mitrajez* 1980) MMG is the Yugoslavian copy of the Soviet PK. Despite its "1980" designation, the weapon doesn't seem to have been fielded until the mid-1980s, suggesting that there may have been problems in perfecting the design or with manufacturing techniques.

As with the PK, the M80 can be used with a bipod or tripod mount and has a quick-change barrel with a carrying handle. The stock has a distinctive shape quite different from that of the Soviet PK.

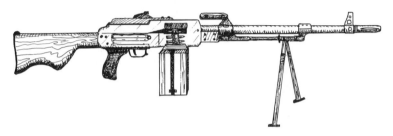

The Yugoslavian M80 (*Mitrajez* 1980) MMG is a copy of the Soviet PK. The M80 can be used with a bipod or tripod mount and has a quick-change barrel with a carrying handle.

Specifications for AK-Based Machine Guns

Name	Barrel Length (inches)	Weight (unloaded) (pounds)	Length (inches)	Magazine Capacity
Chinese Type 81	23.2	11	41	75
Chinese RPKS-75 (export)	21	9.5	38.8	75
East German LMG-K	23.2	11	41	40 or 75
Finland M78	22	10.38	41.73	20 or 75
Israeli Galil ARM	18.1	8.5	38.6	35
Romanian RPK	23.2	11	41	40 or 75
Romanian PK	26	19.75	47	100-, 200-, or 300- round belts

Name	Barrel Length (inches)	Weight (unloaded) (pounds)	Length (inches)	Magazine Capacity
Soviet RPK	23.2	11	41	40 or 75
Soviet RPK74	24 *	11 *	42 *	40 or 75
Soviet PK	26	19.75	47	100-, 200-, or 300- round belts
Soviet PKM	26	18.45	47	100-, 200-, or 300- round belts
Vietnamese TUL-1	23.2	11	41	30 or 75
Yugoslavian M65A	20	12.3	41.5	30 or 75
Yugoslavian M65B	20	11.4	41.5	30 or 75
Yugoslavian M72	21.25	11.13	40.35	30 or 75
Yugoslavian M77B1	19.6	11.4	40.6	30
Yugoslavian M80	26	22	46.2	100- or 250- round belt

* Approximate specifications

Chapter 5

⊛ ——————————————————————— ⊛

Owning a Kalashnikov

Kalashnikov rifles are noted for their reliability and durability. This is partially due to the heavy bolt carrier, but other design features also play a part. One of the most important of these is simplicity: the Kalashnikov design does away with numerous parts found in many other rifles and helps keep the firearm's mechanism simple.

For example, the reciprocating charging handle located on the right side of the receiver can be used as a forward assist; a separate device is unnecessary. Likewise, the safety/selector of the Kalashnikov rifles doubles as an ejection port cover, and the bolt hold-open device, which is convenient but not essential, is completely missing from most Kalashnikovs. These simplifications of the basic rifle do away with nine to eleven parts normally incorporated into similar firearms.

The Kalashnikov's simple design also translates into a lower price tag, especially compared to many Western designs. High-tech niceties like 3-round burst modes, aluminum or plastic receivers or trigger parts, telescopic aiming systems, or long barrels are not found on infantry versions of the Kalashnikov, though longer barrels and optical sights are placed on sniper or SAW versions.

Unfortunately, there's a flip side to the Kalashnikov's simplicity. The human engineering (how "user friendly" the rifle is) leaves much to be desired in several areas. Good examples of this are found in the very points that translate into manufacturing pluses: the safety is noisy, slow, and hard to operate; the lack of a bolt hold-open device makes minor cleaning or quick reloading difficult; the rear sight is not nearly as quick to use as a peep sight and is exposed to jars and knocks; and the rifle's heaviness makes it hard for a user to carry as much ammunition as his less heavily burdened counterpart.

Of course, many human engineering problems can be overcome through practice, tricks of various sorts, or modification of the rifle. For example, one can overcome the lack of a bolt hold-open device by loading several tracer rounds at the bottom of the magazine and then topping it off with standard rounds. When the shooter sees a tracer, he knows it's time to change magazines. (In combat, some may want to add a tracer at the top of the magazine to keep enemies confused as to whether the special rounds are at the top or bottom of the magazine.)

Likewise, the open "V" or notch sight found on most communist-made rifles can be easily modified by a gunsmith, or a Western version like the Valmet or Galil may be selected which has a rear peep sight. Optical sights or rifle scopes can be mounted using a scope mount like those offered for the Galil rifles or from B-Square.

Those wishing to get around the unfriendly Kalashnikov selector can purchase a Galil and have a thumb-control lever nearly as handy as that of the AR-15 (and which lefties can activate with the forefinger) or just leave the safety in the fire position and keep the trigger finger clear of the trigger until firing. Even the "Kalashnikov clack" of the selector can be minimized through the field expedient of bending the selector up and away from the receiver ever so slightly and placing a small piece of plastic tape on its underside. (Be sure to replace the tape from time to time.)

The human engineering of the Kalashnikov isn't all bad. The front sight is a single post with a protective ring or "dog ears," depending on the model; either of these arrangements can be used to give a lead on moving targets (if the shooter is very familiar with his rifle) and can also help to quickly locate the front sight when bringing it to bear on a target. The rifle is short and handy; the folding-stock version is as short as nearly any Western "shorty" rifle, and considerably shorter than all standard rifles except for bullpup designs.

Kalashnikov rifles are also very easy to strip and maintain; a shooter can strip a Kalashnikov down to its basic components without special tools; the gas tube and piston are as easy to clean as the bore. This ease of cleaning pays off in a more reliable rifle as well as one that lasts longer than those which are used with dirt and grit in them because field stripping them is a chore the user foregoes whenever possible.

Even the Kalashnikov's weight is not without its good points. The weight makes control in automatic or very rapid semiauto fire considerably easier than with lighter rifles. And certainly the rifle's weight is brought about in part by the robustness of its parts. A rifle which doesn't fail in combat has to be seen as more user friendly than the high-tech wonder that clutches at a critical moment; heavy steel parts are usually less apt to break, all things being equal, than their plastic or aluminum counterparts.

Other very sound design features of the Kalashnikov are the charging handle and magazine release positions. Magazines can be quickly changed with either hand by using the off-hand thumb tip to push the release while grasping the magazine with the fingers and base of the thumb. The rocking action needed to seat the magazine in the well ensures that magazines are easily inserted and seated.

Chrome plating of the barrel and chamber and the use of a stainless-steel gas piston make Kalashnikov rifles easier to clean as well as stronger and more resistant to corrosion.

The sheer number and variety of Kalashnikov rifles is a major plus for those needing similar rifles for several different purposes. With rifles available chambered for 5.56mm/.223 Remington, 7.62mm NATO/.308 Winchester, and 7.62x39mm, as well as training rifles chambered for the .22 LR, many shooters have discovered that they can create an off-the-shelf family of weapons which operate similarly and may even enjoy some interchangeable parts. Thus, a shooter can own a family of rifles capable of fulfilling a wide variety of hunting or combat roles without having to "relearn" how to operate or field strip whatever gun he needs for the job at hand.

Having weapons with identical operating features can be especially important when the critical moment comes in hunting or combat. Falling back on habits developed on a rifle with a different style of safety, sighting system, or trigger pull often spells disaster for a shooter if the gun in his hands operates differently. He may fumble for a safety where there is none or be distracted by an unfamiliar trigger pull. Having a weapon identical to the others he often uses avoids such problems; the variety of Kalashnikov rifles makes such a collection of firearms possible.

While the operation of the various Kalashnikovs is virtually identical, some features are quite dissimilar. The folding-stock mechanisms can vary greatly from one model to the next. In general, the AKS47 and AKMS versions of the weapon have a large release button located just above the pistol grip on the left side of the receiver. When the stock is released, it folds under the rifle.

Other stocks are more rigid. The Valmet and Galil folding stocks have very tight lockups but are harder to release from their extended positions. The folding stock release button of the AKS74 is on the left side of the rear of the receiver but, unlike earlier Soviet-designed AK stocks, folds to the left and is held in place by a spring-loaded hook. The release button on the Chinese side-folding stocks is on the top right of the mechanism; the release locks the stock in either the open or closed position; the stock folds to the right side of the receiver.

Regardless which version a shooter has, it is possible to become very proficient in operating the rifle with practice. Once the shooter gains skill in operating his rifle, he'll discover that it very seldom fails him if cared for properly.

Field Stripping and Cleaning

Like any other rifle, the Kalashnikov will start to show adverse wear or malfunction if it isn't kept reasonably clean. Fortunately, the rifle is easy to field strip, and cleaning isn't much of a chore.

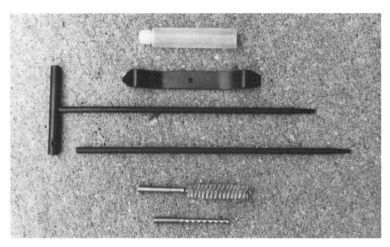

Most Kalashnikovs come with excellent cleaning kits. Shown here is the standard Valmet kit which is normally carried in web equipment rather than stored on the rifle itself.

Field stripping a Kalashnikov requires no special tools. This rifle is nearly field stripped (with only the removal of the gas tube left to be done). This Chinese Kalashnikov has a cleaning kit in its stock and a cleaning rod under its barrel.

The Kalashnikov requires no special maintenance tools. Although a tool is available to adjust the front sight, the sight can easily be adjusted with a drift punch (windage) and needle-nosed pliers can zero the elevation of the front sight post. In the case of rifles with a complete ring around the front sight, a special wrench is also helpful; such a tool can be easily fabricated from an old screwdriver with a notch cut into its blade. Even when detailed stripping is called for to disassemble the trigger group or other parts of the rifle, the only tools needed are needle-nosed pliers, drift punches and mallets, and a set of screwdrivers.

Field stripping and cleaning require only a cleaning kit which, with many versions of the rifle, will have its rod located under the barrel and brushes and other gear in the storage compartment inside the stock (accessed through the butt plate).

The following procedure should be used to field strip the rifle for cleaning:

1) Remove the magazine and cycle the action, checking the chamber of the rifle to be sure it's empty.

2) Push in the retaining lever on the rear of the receiver cover, and lift the receiver cover up and back to remove it.

3) Take out the action spring and retaining rod by pushing them forward to release them, then lift them up slightly and back them out of the receiver.

4) Remove the bolt and bolt carrier (which will also have the gas piston attached to it) by pulling them back and out.

5) Take the bolt out of the carrier by twisting the bolt counterclockwise and pulling it out of the front of the carrier.

6) Remove the gas cylinder by pulling it backward and lifting it out.

This will give access to the bore and gas cylinder so that they can be quickly cleaned. When cleaning the rifle, care should be taken with the gas piston; the magazine and trigger group should be checked for debris. If the magazine is disassembled for cleaning, great care should be taken to note how the spring is aligned so that it can be replaced properly. Reassembly of the Kalashnikovs is simply a reversal of the procedure.

Even if a Kalashnikov hasn't been fired for a while, it is wise to give the mechanism a good cleaning if dirt or sand may have gotten into it. While the rifle will probably function without a hitch in such a condition, grit can cause excessive wear. A clean weapon lasts longer and is less apt to fail.

The Kalashnikov's already somewhat marginal accuracy can be ruined by improper cleaning techniques. One poor practice is to allow the cleaning rod to rub against the bore. To minimize this, clean the barrel from the breech rather than the muzzle. Even so, be especially careful with the cleaning rod; do not allow it to scrape against the last of the rifling, which determines just how straight the bullet leaving the gun will travel.

If the Kalashnikov comes with a steel cleaning rod, use it. Aluminum cleaning rods should be avoided or kept religiously clean to keep them from picking up bits of grit which can cut into the metal of the bore during cleaning. Pull-through string cleaning rods work if care is taken not to use too large a cleaning patch; once a patch gets jammed in the barrel with one of these cleaning strings, it usually means a trip to the gunsmith. Trying to shoot out a patch will rupture the barrel — don't try it. The old jokes about troops ruining their rifles when the buttons on the shirt they were using as a cleaning patch got caught in the bore are real funny — until *you* get a patch caught in the bore. Better to be safe than sorry when using a pull-through cleaning kit.

If a rifle lacks a cleaning rod, U.S. military-surplus steel rods are ideal and readily available from mail-order companies like Sierra Supply or Sherwood International.

Cleaning fluids and lubricants abound. Break-Free CLP is probably the best lubricant and cleaner available. This material was created for the U.S. military rifles and can be used over a wide temperature range; it also does away with having to use a bore-cleaning solvent and a lubricating oil, since Break-Free CLP does both jobs.

One important practice when using Break-Free CLP is to let the rifle sit for half an hour or so after cleaning since it takes a while for the lubricants to set up and offer their full lubrication. Most gun stores carry Break-Free CLP as well as a wealth of other lubricants.

Sometimes a dry lubricant is preferable over oils which can congeal in cold weather or collect dust and grit in dirty environments. First choice of these is E & L Manufacturing's Gun Lube. Other dry lubricants are also available at gun stores.

Whatever type of lubricant you choose, use it sparingly, since too much will collect dirt over time. The gas tube should be treated gently since a ding or even deep scratches can cause problems. Experts disagree as to whether the gas tube and piston should be lubricated; a few recommend that a light coat of oil be applied to the gas piston. I personally feel that *no* oil should be used in the gas tube since many oils can create scale in the tube when it becomes hot. If a high-temperature lubricant is used in the gas tube or on the gas piston, use only the most minimal amounts. When the piston is chromed, there is no reason to use a lubricant since the metal tends to be self-lubricating.

When cleaning is finished, the rifle's bore should be carefully checked to be sure it's clear of patch threads and oil. Any material left in the barrel can ruin it with just one shot. Avoid getting cleaning fluids or oils on wooden stocks, as many such products can gradually stain the wood or even damage it. If oiled stocks need to be treated, linseed oil is generally the material of choice. Stocks which are excessively dirty or coated with packing grease or the like can often be cleaned up with a light coating of paint remover on a rag. Take care not to remove too much of the stock's oil in this process; reoiling wooden furniture with linseed oil may still be necessary even if great care is taken.

With Kalashnikovs having a baked enamel or paint finish on exterior parts, no oil is needed unless bare metal is shining through. Another coat of paint would be the best bet, though touch-up blue can be used to darken the metal. Oil can be placed over the bare metal to protect it in a pinch, but doing so will cause the gun to attract dirt when used outdoors. On blued or parkerized rifles, a light coating of oil on the exterior of the firearm is necessary to prevent rust. Take care to wipe off fingerprints periodically from these finishes, and apply a new light coat of oil from time to time.

Too much oil on internal parts can create problems; a thick coat of fluid doesn't improve lubricating properties and may actually cause excessive wear if grit becomes trapped in it.

Because oil can quickly deactivate ammunition and since chromed metal can't corrode or rust, rifles with chromed chambers and bores can be left dry without any lubrication inside the bore after they've been cleaned. Once the rifle has been cleaned, a dry cleaning patch should be run down the bore to leave it clean and ready to fire.

Care should also be taken that the magazine and magazine well are not oily, since this lubricant will deactivate the cartridges if they remain in the magazine for a while. While most cartridges are sealed tightly, they still shouldn't be handled with oily hands, and oil should never be used to lubricate a cartridge for better chambering or the like. This is a dangerous practice even if the cartridge isn't deactivated, since it can create excessive recoil pressures against the bolt upon firing.

When a Kalashnikov is stored for several months or more, it should not be placed in a leather or plastic container. Such a container will collect moisture inside and can ruin a rifle in a very short time. Instead, a firearm should always be put into a container that breathes, such as a cardboard box or woven burlap gun case. Even if a rifle is stored in a suitable container, it should still be cleaned at least twice a year and more often in high-humidity areas. The only time to store a gun in an air-tight container is after the gun has been packed in grease (or the like) and a dessicant placed in the container to take moisture out of the air.

The barrel life of any rifle (and the Kalashnikovs are no exception) will be greatly shortened if long strings of shots are fired without letting the barrel cool. While this isn't normally a concern, it should be kept in mind for those doing a lot of combat-style practice. Letting the barrel cool between strings of shots will help it last much longer.

One potential problem with Kalashnikovs which see rugged use is the exposed end of the gas tube (or the whole exposed gas tube on rifles like the Galil and Valmet). One good dent in this tube and the gas rod will start binding, and the rifle won't function well, if at all. Even though such an accident is rare, care should be taken to protect this portion of the rifle.

Complete Disassembly

When doing extensive work on a firearm, work on a surface which is soft enough that it won't scratch the metal. It is also wise to work where the light is good and where parts won't be easily lost. Having a container for small parts during disassembly of the rifle is a good idea. Egg cartons, ice cube trays, small jars, or similar containers work well for this.

In general, it is best not to disassemble a firearm any more than is really necessary to clean it or repair or replace a part. Even then, it is seldom necessary to disassemble the rifle beyond the field stripping stage. Every time a firearm is disassembled beyond this point, it will take some time for some parts to regain their fit; some may tend to shake loose with firing after being disassembled; better to skip any unnecessary disassembly steps than risk such problems in the future.

Some parts of most Kalashnikov rifles are riveted together. Repairing these can be quite a hassle, since the end of the rivet has to be ground off, the parts removed, and the new or repaired parts installed with a new rivet which must be carefully set to secure them while not causing damage. Fortunately, most parts fastened in place with rivets seldom break.

Ideally, the disassembly steps listed below will *not* be carried out by anyone other than a competent gunsmith. A lot of damage can be done if disassembly is attempted without the proper know-how. However, in a survival or combat situation, where not having an operating firearm is a life-or-death situation, trying to carry out such work might be justified. The costs will have to be weighed in such a case. That said, the best rule of thumb is: *do not tackle any type of gunsmithing work or disassembly beyond field stripping unless you are qualified to do it.*

Before disassembling a rifle, study the assembled rifle so that you can more easily reassemble it. The owner's manual is also very useful (especially any exploded diagrams) in showing the parts relationships.

That said, to disassemble a Kalashnikov rifle, first carry out the field stripping as outlined in the previous section. Once this is done, carry out the following additional steps as needed to get to the part which needs to be replaced or repaired:

7) The extractor and extractor spring are held in place by the large pin (which may be a solid or roll pin, depending on the rifle) located on the side of the bolt near the locking lugs. Before trying to drift out this pin, check to be sure one side isn't staked; if it is, go out the other side opposite the staked spot in the bolt. Drift the pin out with a drift punch or small nail to free the extractor. Take care, since the spring is under tension.

Side view of bolt carrier and gas piston with bolt still in place.

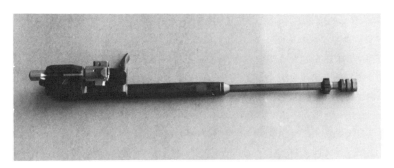

Bottom view of bolt carrier and piston with bolt in place.

8) The smaller pin located on the side of the bolt near the locking lugs retains the firing pin (and its spring on models with a firing-pin spring); note whether the pin is staked in place. Drifting the pin out frees the firing pin; take care, since this spring is also under pressure.

Front view of the bolt.

Side view of the bolt.

9) The gas piston is held to the bolt-carrier extension arm by a roll pin. This pin should be drifted out only if the piston needs to be repaired or replaced, since damage to the piston can occur during this process.

10) Flash hiders or muzzle nuts are sometimes held in place by a pin, but usually are screwed onto the barrel; some Kalashnikov rifles lack them entirely. On Valmet rifles, the cross pin should be driven out from left to

right (the right side of the rifle is the side with the ejection port).

11) The gas port block is generally held in place by cross pins; don't remove it unless absolutely necessary, as this can be a tedious process on some rifles and it may be hard to replace it so it stays in place. Pins are generally drifted out from the left of the rifle to its right. Should an obstruction of the tunnel of the gas port occur, note that the tunnel doesn't run perpendicular to the barrel; rather, it is slanted diagonally with its rear end toward the gas tube and its lower, forward end over the porting hole in the rifle's barrel.

12) The fore grip may be attached to the rifle in a variety of ways; the method for removal is best deter-

The fore grip on this Valmet is held in place by a threaded plate which requires a special wrench for removal, though it can be drifted loose with a punch. Fore grips should be left in place unless removal is absolutely necessary.

mined by studying the rifle. On the Valmet rifles, the grip is held in place by a threaded plate which requires a special wrench for removal, though it can be drifted loose with a punch.

13) The trigger group's pins are released by removing the looped retaining spring on the left inside of the receiver on semiauto rifles, or the long leg of the disconnector spring on selective-fire guns.

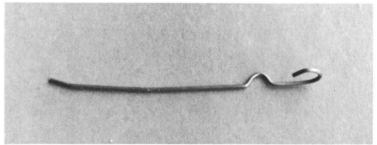

Shown here is the looped retaining spring which holds the trigger group's pins on semiauto Kalashnikovs.

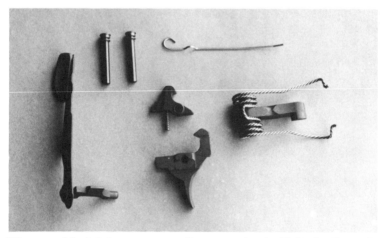

Disassembled trigger group from semiauto Kalashnikov. At left is selector; hammer and trigger pins and their retaining spring are shown at top. In center is the sear and its spring with the trigger below it. Hammer and its spring are to the right.

Before freeing the spring or leg, place the selector in the fire position, and, while restraining the hammer, pull the trigger. Hold the hammer and carefully lower it until it is fully forward, facedown. This done, the retaining spring can be pulled forward and out by grasping its loop with a pair of needle-nosed pliers and pulling forward and out.

Kalashnikov hammer and its braided-wire spring (front view).

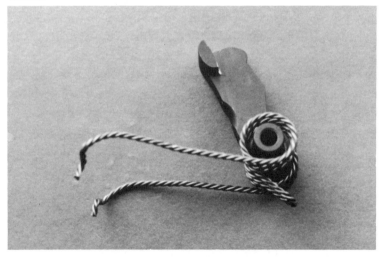

Kalashnikov hammer and its braided-wire spring (side view).

On selective-fire rifles, the long leg of the disconnector spring should be pulled up to free the disconnector pin; remove the pin out the left side of the receiver and then take out the disconnector (also sometimes called the auto sear) and its spring to free the other parts of the trigger group.

 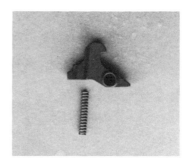

The trigger and sear shown in their assembled positions(left). A slave pin should be used to hold the sear and its spring in place on the trigger during reassembly. At right, the Kalashnikov sear and its spring.

14) Once the retaining spring is removed, the trigger group is freed by sliding the hammer and trigger pins out the left side of the receiver. This will free the hammer and its spring, which can be removed by turning them slightly and lifting them out. Next, the trigger and sear can be removed, along with the rate reducer and its spring on Soviet-style rifles; take care not to lose the sear spring which sits between the sear and trigger.

15) If the safety/selector needs to be removed, rotate its forward end upward so that it can be pulled out the right side of the receiver.

16) Most stocks are held in place by screws or (with many folding stocks) by pins. Do not remove the stock unless absolutely necessary for repair or replacement.

17) The magazine release and its spring are held in

place with a rivet. Don't remove them unless absolutely necessary.

18) Pistol grips are generally held in place by a bolt which can be unscrewed through the open base of the grip. Don't remove the grip unless absolutely necessary.

19) The front sight post generally screws into its base. The sight assembly can be removed by drifting; a set screw or screws may need to be loosened first. The front sight should not be removed unless absolutely necessary since a tight fit helps keep it zeroed.

20) The rear sight is generally pinned or screwed into place with its base welded onto the rifle. Don't remove the rear sight unless absolutely necessary; note the way the leaf spring under the sight is aligned so that it can be properly reassembled. Great care should be taken with front and rear sights containing tritium; while this material is safe in the containers mounted on the rifles, breaking one will release the radioactive material into the atmosphere. Should this happen, the rifle should immediately be taken out into the open air and the room where the break occurred aired out for twenty-four hours to allow the radioactive gas to escape. The rifle should then be sent back to the factory for repair. Tritium gradually decays so that it will become rather dim in ten to fifteen years and need to be replaced; again, this is a job for the factory.

Reassembly is basically the reversal of the above procedures. If the trigger group has been disassembled, the selector should go in before the other parts, followed by the trigger and sear. A slave pin should be used to hold the sear and its spring (and the rate reducer and its spring on Soviet-style AKMs) in place on the trigger; the slave pin is then pushed out the right side of the receiver when the trigger retaining pin is inserted. When the trigger group is in place, cock the hammer before trying to replace the bolt carrier.

During reassembly, a minimum of force should be needed to get the rifle back together. Excessive force means something isn't assembled in its correct position and will damage the part or make the assembled rifle inoperable at best. Take the time to reassemble the rifle correctly.

Avoiding Potential Problems

While malfunctions of a Kalashnikov rifle are rare when it's kept clean, problems can occur. Most problems are caused by excessive fouling, poor ammunition, or a damaged magazine. Cleaning the rifle, changing ammunition, or replacing the magazine will generally clear up most troubles a shooter may have.

If problems persist, the best thing to do is to take the rifle to a good gunsmith. However, in a survival or combat situation, the shooter may not have this luxury, and continued malfunctions may spell grave danger. If such use is anticipated, any problems with the rifle or with parts which show excessive wear should be dealt with *before* the rifle becomes completely unserviceable. A spare parts kit (more about this in a subsequent chapter) would be wise to have if lives may depend on the continued functioning of the Kalashnikov.

To prevent excessive wear, "hot" ammunition should be avoided whenever possible. Hot loads don't add all that much in velocity or capability, especially in the short standard-length Kalashnikov rifles, and a diet of hot loads in a firearm will greatly shorten its life.

If reloads are used, great care should be taken to be sure they are not overloaded. With the huge number of countries producing 7.62x39mm, 5.56mm/.223, and .308

Winchester ammunition, the shooter must take pains in reloading, since the brass thickness of a cartridge can vary greatly from one manufacturer to another. A thick brass case translates to smaller interior capacity, which can raise what would normally be a safe powder load to dangerous pressures; reloaders should approach maximum loads with great caution when using military or foreign brass.

Excessive loads or poor ammunition can be extremely dangerous with a Kalashnikov. Should the bolt fail, a round fire prematurely, or a bolt be partly opened and a hangfire occur, the thin sheet-metal receiver cover won't give much protection to the shooter, especially when compared to a rifle with a metal upper receiver. In such a mishap, much of the hot gas and case fragments could make their way to the shooter's face. Avoid using reloads or other ammunition of unknown or dubious history. (The old saying, "My face may be ugly but I take care of it because it's the best face I have," applies here.)

Reloads or other ammunition which are too light can also create real problems, since they'll fail to cycle a Kalashnikov. This is a small inconvenience in hunting or plinking but may be fatal if the rifle is used for self-defense. Therefore, before purchasing several thousand reloads or cranking them out with a reloading press, or buying a crate of military surplus ammunition that may have aged in the hot sun on a dock in some banana republic somewhere, try out the ammunition in *your* rifle to be sure it will function properly.

One point for those who reload: Be sure that cannelured bullets have been used and that the lips of the brass have been crimped so that the bullets can't be shoved back into the cartridge during chambering. With non-cannelured bullets, the Kalashnikov's heavy bolt can shove the bullet into the cartridge case with alarming regularity. Firing a round in such a state is asking for severe damage, since dangerous pressure levels are created by the powder compression and/or lessening of air space in the brass cartridge when the bullet is pushed into it.

One way to avoid unneeded cleaning problems is to abstain from using corrosive ammunition. If you must use such noxious stuff, be sure to clean the rifle immediately to prevent possible corrosion and rusting of various parts of the firearm. The old method of pouring a solution of boiling hot water and soda or soap down the barrel to get rid of corrosive residue isn't necessary with chromed bores but might be a good idea with the rare versions of the Kalashnikov which lack them. Ideally, shooters would avoid altogether communist-made ammunition which uses corrosive primers.

The best bet with ammunition is to purchase it from a reputable company like Olin/Winchester or Federal Cartridge Company; Hansen and PMC are first choice for imported ammunition. All these companies sell new, quality ammunition loaded to military specifications; Winchester's USA line, Federal's "American Eagle" brand, and PMC's standard "ball" ammunition are competitively priced, so that shooters should have no need to resort to inferior corrosive ammunition.

Kalashnikovs which have been used for a while generally function just a bit better than brand-new ones. Like most machinery, firearms come from the factory with some rough edges and bearing surfaces which don't match perfectly. These quickly wear down as the weapon is used; after several hundred rounds have gone through a firearm, it will often custom-fit its parts and function very reliably. Consequently, any rifle which must function at peak reliability should be taken out and test-fired with several hundred rounds to break it in.

One source of problems with a Kalashnikov is do-it-yourself gunsmith work. No one should tackle even a simple gunsmithing job unless he knows exactly what he's doing. The same idea applies to the purchase of accessories: they shouldn't be bought unless they are *really* needed. Accessories can quickly mess things up and seem to have a synergistic effect in their ability to cause problems rather than alleviate them.

Troubleshooting

If a Kalashnikov rifle fails to fire, there are some quick steps that the shooter should go through.

1) He should first tap the magazine to be sure it is seated.

2) Next, he should pull back on the charging lever, holding it back while he checks that a case is ejected, and be sure a shell isn't jammed in the weapon or still in the chamber.

3) If the chamber is clear, he should release the charging handle to chamber a new round. He should *not* "ride" the bolt forward to see if a round has been chambered; rather, he can pull back slightly on the bolt to check. He should then be sure the bolt is again fully seated.

4) Next, he should check the safety to be sure the rifle is ready to fire.

5) Now the shooter should again aim and try to fire his rifle.

6) If the rifle fails to fire, he should go through steps 1 through 5 one more time.

7) If his rifle still fails to function, he should remove the magazine, cycle the weapon to be sure it's empty, and check the inside of the rifle through the ejection port and magazine well, while he holds back the bolt. This may reveal dirt or a broken part.

8) If he still hasn't found the fault, he should change magazines or inspect the one in use if others aren't available, cycle the action, and try firing again.

9) If the fault still isn't apparent, he should field strip the rifle, if practical, and try to locate the problem.

Despite these steps and the care a shooter takes in keeping his Kalashnikov clean and well maintained, his rifle may still fail to function. If a shooter is just using the rifle for plinking or hunting, he should take it to a gunsmith for repair.

In a combat or survival situation, it may be a different story. Then, knowing how to get the rifle functioning again may mean the difference between life and death. If so, a shooter would do well to read and study the procedures below so that he will know what to do if he should have to try to get his rifle into firing condition on his own.

The reader is cautioned, however, not to carry out any of these procedures unless failing to do so would endanger life, since the following procedures are dangerous in and of themselves. If a life isn't on the line, no attempt to carry out the actual measures should be made with live ammunition. The best way to get a firearm fixed is to take it to a gunsmith. The reader must understand: *The following procedures can be very dangerous and should only be attempted when not having a functioning firearm puts a life in more jeopardy than would a possible mishap with the firearm.*

Note also that there are slight differences in some

parts and among the various series and models of the Kalashnikov rifles. Some of these steps may not apply to a specific weapon.

Troubleshooting Procedures

Problem	Check For	Procedure
Bolt won't unlock	Dirty or burred bolt	Clean or replace
	Damaged gas tube or piston	Repair or replace
Bolt won't lock	Fouling in locking lugs	Clean and lubricate lugs
	Frozen extractor (in down position)	Remove and clean extractor
	Recoil spring is not moving freely	Remove, clean, and lubricate
	Bolt is not moving freely	Remove, clean, and lubricate
	Gas piston misaligned	Check alignment; replace or realign
	Loose or damaged piston	Tighten or replace
	Dent in gas tube	Repair or replace
Double feeding	Defective magazine	Replace

Problem	Check For	Procedure
Firearm won't cock; selector doesn't work properly	Worn, broken, or missing parts	Check parts, replace
Firearm continues to fire after release of trigger	Dirt in trigger/sear	Clean mechanism
	Broken sear/trigger	Replace
	Weak sear/trigger spring	Replace spring
	Firing pin dirty or too long	Clean or replace
Firearm won't fire	Safety in safe position	Place in fire position
	Firing pin is broken	Replace
	Too much oil or dirt in firing pin recess	Wipe/clean
	Poor ammo	Remove/discard
	Weak or broken hammer or hammer spring	Replace
	Weak or broken sear or sear spring	Replace
	Bolt isn't locking	Clean dirty parts

Problem	Check For	Procedure
Round won't chamber	Dirty or corroded ammo	Clean ammo
	Damaged ammo	Replace
	Fouling in chamber	Clean chamber
Rounds won't eject	Broken ejector	Replace
	Frozen ejector	Clean/lubricate
	Bad ejector spring	Replace
Rounds won't extract	Broken extractor or bad extractor spring	Replace
	Dirty/corroded ammo	Remove (may have to be carefully pushed out with cleaning rod); *use extreme caution with live round*
	Carbon/fouling in chamber or extractor lip	Clean chamber and lip
	Dirty/faulty recoil spring	Clean/replace
Rounds won't feed	Dirty or corroded ammo	Clean off ammo

Problem	Check For	Procedure
Rounds won't feed (cont.)	Low-powered ammo	Use different ammo
	Defective magazine	Replace magazine
	Dirt in magazine	Clean and lubricate magazine
	Too many rounds in magazine	Remove several rounds
	Insufficient gas to cycle action fully	Clean out gas port, gas rod, etc. (If gun has adjustable gas port, check setting)
	Magazine not seated	Reseat/replace magazine
	Broken magazine catch	Repair/replace
Selector lever binds	Fouling/lack of lubrication	Lubricate; if it still binds, disassemble and clean
Short recoil (new rounds fail to chamber)	Poor ammunition	Replace
	Fouling in gas port	Clean gas port
	Damaged piston	Repair/replace
	Dent in gas tube	Repair or replace

Chapter 6

—————————————————————————

Ammunition

There is a real wealth of ammunition to choose from when it comes to stoking the Kalashnikov rifles. The standard Kalashnikov rifles are chambered for 7.62x 39mm; the machine gun and sniper versions are chambered for larger rounds; rifles aimed at the Western export market are chambered for 5.56mm/.223 Remington and .308 Winchester; and .22 rimfire versions are available (covered in the next chapter).

In addition to military and "military-style" ammunition, there is a wide array of sporting ammunition available in these chamberings so that Kalashnikov rifles, although certainly not of the traditional hunting-rifle configuration, are also suitable for harvesting game. (Many of these sporting rounds are also ideal for combat by those not restricted by the conventions of war.)

Shooters in the United States have recently seen a price drop on practice, hunting, and combat ammunition. This developed from the growing popularity of assault-type rifles based on a growing feeling that such weapons might one day be needed to combat crime, to use for survival purposes, or even to repel an invasion of the United States. Whether these needs were real or

113

not, these rifles, with their high-capacity magazines and the high firepower tactics often used with them, created a huge market for low-priced ammunition. This need was first filled by military-style ammunition imported from Eastern Europe and China.

Currently, U.S. companies like Winchester, with its USA ammunition, and Federal Cartridge Company, with its American Eagle brand, are gaining a share of this market by offering ammunition that is virtually identical to what they make for the U.S. military. This American-made ammunition is competitively priced and has the additional plus of being easily reloadable and non-corrosive.

This growing market, coupled with the wide variety of Kalashnikov chamberings, has made a huge and ever-changing array of ammunition available. With this in mind, here is a sampling of the wide variety of available ammunition in the United States.

.22 Short

Neither the .22 trainers nor any variant of the Kalashnikov is chambered for this round. It can be used in .22 LR rifles, but isn't too satisfactory for such use; even though it will chamber, it will not cycle a semiauto action and, with extensive, prolonged use, might cause chamber erosion. This, coupled with a price tag that is usually higher than the .22 LR, makes it a poor choice.

Some shooters occasionally use the .22 Short in .22 LR guns because the report produced is relatively soft in the long barrel of a rifle. A much better choice for quiet shooting is the .22 CB Long Cap (see below), since it is even softer and won't produce barrel erosion.

.22 Long

The .22 Long is between the .22 Short and .22 LR in power. Like the .22 Short, the .22 Long will chamber in a .22 LR trainer. Since it lacks the accuracy of the .22 LR and won't consistently cycle the action of most semi-auto guns, it is also an inferior choice.

.22 CB Long Cap

Back in the early 1900s, the .22 CB Cap was often used in shooting galleries where its soft report and low velocity made it ideal. CCI revived the idea in the early 1970s as its .22 CB Long Cap with one important change: the cartridge is now the size of the Long Rifle, making it possible to use it in guns chambered for that cartridge without chambering problems or chamber erosion problems. This also makes for a lower price tag on this ammunition, since CCI uses its standard brass cases to make the .22 CB Cap.

In 1988, Federal Cartridge Company followed CCI's lead and created its own version, the .22 Long CB Cap. The two rounds are nearly identical; both use a 29-grain lubricated lead bullet with low muzzle velocity and minimal report.

The big plus of the .22 CB Long Cap (of either manufacturer) is that it can be used in a .22 rifle without ear protection. In fact, it allows nearly silent shooting; the clatter of the hammer falling makes more noise than the retort except for those toward the front of the muzzle where the sound is more readily heard. The .22 CB Long Cap doesn't cycle the action of a .22 semiauto rifle; rounds are chambered by cycling the action by hand (making the rifle a sort of bolt-action gun). This can be ideal for training beginners, since it makes the accidental second shot that can occur with semiauto rifles in a beginner's hands nearly impossible.

The .22 CB Long Cap is also quite useful for making silent shots at varmints and for indoor or backyard practice (with an adequate backstop). The round changes a standard .22 rifle into the ballistic equivalent of a super air gun. The 29-grain bullet of the .22 CB Long leaves the barrel of a firearm at 727 fps (feet per second). Taking into consideration the greater weight of the projectile being fired, this makes the .22 with a .22 CB Long Cap superior in power to commercial air guns currently offered.

The .22 CB Long is a round that can make a Kalashnikov-style .22 training rifle a lot more versatile. When purchasing the .22 CB Long Cap, care should be taken not to get the shorter .22 CB Short which has a cartridge the size of the .22 Short.

.22 Long Rifle

Originally loaded with black powder, the .22 LR was developed in 1887 and is found in nearly every country of the world, with billions of rounds cranked out each year. This universality has created a huge number of firearms chambered for the round, now loaded with smokeless powder in its modern reincarnations, including several training rifles modeled to look like the Kalashnikov rifle. The case on the standard .22 LR round is the same length as that of the .22 Long, but the bullet—and therefore the overall length of the case—of the .22 LR is greater than that of the weaker cartridge.

A wealth of different types of ammunition gives the owner of a .22 LR firearm the ability to select ammunition to suit many different purposes in addition to training and practice use. In a pinch, the hypervelocity rounds might even be used for taking medium-sized game or for self-defense, though they are not ideal for such use since they don't give reliable results quickly enough.

CCI's Stinger is currently the best .22 LR round for hunting game at the large end of the "small game" scale. The Stinger has a slightly longer than normal case which allows more slow-burning powder to be packed into it; its 32-grain bullet is smaller than standard .22 bullets, giving it a higher speed than would otherwise result with its powder charge. These two innovations give its bullet higher velocity and make it expand reliably to expend its energy within most small game rather than penetrating through it. Of course, this devastating power can also destroy a lot of meat on small animals; for very small game, solid point .22 bullets are better suited.

Remington, Federal, and Winchester produce rounds similar to the Stinger. These rounds are marketed as hypervelocity ammunition; they're hypervelocity only when compared to other .22 LR ammunition. Their speeds are still within the ranges of pistol bullets (as opposed to the high-velocity designation normally used for rifle bullets traveling at speeds faster than 2,000 to 2,500 fps).

One might imagine that these cartridges would be superior to the old-style, heavy lead .22 bullets at longer ranges. But this isn't the case, since light bullets lose their speed faster than heavier bullets. Hypervelocity bullets peter out at around 80 to 100 yards; the heavier bullets maintain a greater speed beyond this range which translates into more power.

Another family of .22 LR ammunition is the "high velocity" type (again, this is high velocity only when compared to older-style .22 ammunition and shouldn't be confused with high-velocity centerfire rifle ammunition.) This type of ammunition generally has a hollow-point bullet and a metallic jacket over the lead bullet to reduce barrel fouling. It is ideal for many types of target shooting as well as hunting. These rounds are also less apt to ricochet than are standard FMJ or lead bullets.

For shooting at the extreme limits of the .22 LR's practical ranges, several types of high-velocity ammunition are quite good. CCI's Mini-Mag LR HS, Federal's Hi-Power, or Winchester's 37-grain HP are all good bets; Winchester's Silhouette ammunition, with a 42-grain lead bullet, is first choice for shooting out to 100 or even 125 yards.

Another type of .22 LR is the "standard" ammunition, which has a rounded lead bullet. This ammunition is inexpensive, which makes it ideal for practice but often less than ideal for many types of hunting. Since the bullets are occasionally a bit loose in the brass and the powder and lubricants apt to foul a rifle with extended use, these rounds are not ideal for use where reliable functioning of the firearm is a must.

Finally, several types of target, or "match," .22 LR are often found. Generally, these are rather expensive and the results they give won't be all that much better than standard ammunition in most trainer/practice rifles. For those wanting to try for extra accuracy, Winchester's R1 Match or Federal's Champion Target ammunition work well in most .22 rifles.

If accuracy is a concern while money is limited, it should be kept in mind that most .22 rifles shoot tighter groups with some brands of ammunition than with others. A shooter would do well to purchase a box of five or six varieties of ammunition and test each type for accuracy and functioning in his rifle. Such results will usually indicate which is best for any given rifle.

Another trick used by some shooters to gain accuracy from their .22 rifles is to weigh .22 ammunition and shoot only rounds which all weigh the same. The theory behind this is that since brass is the most consistently made ammunition component, some cartridges weigh more or less than their fellows because the bullet is a slightly different size or the powder charge isn't right. Removing the oddballs from a pack of ammunition can shrink the size of groups fired by a .22 rifle noticeably.

As mentioned above, the .22 LR is not a self-defense round, but sometimes one has to make do with the weapon at hand. If forced to use the .22 for self-defense, probably the best bet is the high-speed CCI Stinger, which creates a lot of damage to flesh-and-blood targets at ranges within 50 yards; Federal's HP Spitfires and Winchester's SuperMax are both good choices and have ballistics nearly as good as those of the Stinger.

The .22 LR can also give good performance with silencers. Good silencers should be used with standard-velocity .22 LR ammunition for lowest noise signatures. Care must be taken to avoid the hypervelocity .22 ammunition with silenced weapons, since the bullet will make a sonic crack as it leaves the barrel and break the sound barrier (around 1,130 fps at sea level).

.22 Short Magnum

This is an experimental round created by ILARCO (Illinois Arms Company) for its AM-180 rifle. Even though the round is not available commercially at the time of this writing, the gradual increase of power in the .22 LR cartridge would seem to make the .22 Short Magnum the next logical step.

The .22 Short Magnum has the same overall length of the .22 LR cartridge, and when fully developed, will have the power of the .22 WMR (see below). This would allow many rifles currently designed for the .22 LR to be quickly upgraded in power by strengthening their actions somewhat and increasing recoil spring tension and bolt weight. Since many .22 rifles are already overbuilt, they could probably function with the .22 Short Magnum with the simple addition of a heavier recoil spring.

At the time of this writing, the velocity of these rounds is only slightly greater than that of the hypervelocity .22 LR. But should the speed be increased to that of the .22 WMR, and should it become commercially viable, the .22 Short Magnum could prove quite useful for hunting game at the larger end of the small game scale. It might even serve as a self-defense round in a pinch.

.22 Winchester Magnum Rimfire

The .22 WMR is a rather expensive round, compared to other .22 rounds, but offers a bit more power than the .22 LR, making it a good small game round. Several versions of the .22 Kalashnikov-style training rifles are currently chambered for this round.

The .22 WMR is based on the WRF (Winchester RimFire) and was introduced in 1959. The .22 WMR extends the useful range of a rifle used for hunting small game to 100 to 125 yards; the down side of the cartridge is that it is overly destructive of small game at close ranges. In effect, it isn't a replacement for the .22 LR, but a more powerful cartridge suitable for larger types of game or for long-range shooting. This should be kept in mind by those who are trying to choose between the .22 LR and the .22 WMR.

Although the .22 LR will chamber in .22 WMR firearms, this isn't a safe practice and should be avoided. When a .22 LR cartridge is fired in a .22 WMR rifle, the case will rupture and likely become stuck. Even if a shooter could somehow put up with this problem, the .22 WMR bullet has a slightly larger diameter, making .22 LR bullets very inaccurate when fired from a .22 WMR gun.

The .22 WMR hasn't become too popular because of its price and the lack of firearms chambered for it. This translates into fewer types of .22 WMR cartridges to choose from. But there are a few excellent cartridges available: Federal's 50-grain HP .22 WMR ammunition uses a bullet ten grains heavier than other factory offerings, which gives the projectile more momentum at longer ranges. The soft copper jacket on the HP bullet expands somewhat even at its extreme ranges.

5.45x39mm (M74)

Fielded by the Soviet Union in 1974, this round is similar to the U.S. .223 Remington in many respects, though it seems to be inferior in its ability to create wounds.

It appears that the M74's development was spurred by the success of the U.S. .223 Remington in the AR-15 rifle in Vietnam, but it is also possible that the Soviets used much of what they had learned from the creation of the 5.6x39mm (.220 Russian) hunting/target round to create this new combat round.

The M74's standard bullet was apparently designed to become unstable upon impact and to minimize the use of lead. The bullet has a steel jacket with a zinc/

copper alloy coat to protect it from rust. Inside, the bullet has an empty space at its nose with a small lead plug under the space and a steel penetrator below the lead plug. When the bullet strikes tissue, the lead is pressure-formed into the space at the tip of the bullet. This changes the bullet's balance and causes it to tumble; when the lead moves forward in a nonsymmetrical manner, the bullet takes an erratic path. Because of the lead plug's movement, the bullet creates severe wounds even though it doesn't fragment.

Although it is not known what other types of bullet configurations are being made by the Soviet Union in 5.45x39mm, it is likely that tracer and possibly incendiary projectiles are being made. In addition, because the Warsaw Pact is adopting the round, the wide variety of rounds produced by various countries using the 7.62x39mm will undoubtedly be exhibited in the 5.45x 39mm as well.

.223 Remington/M193

Eugene Stoner created the .223 Remington when he was working for Armalite on the AR-15 rifle in the 1950s. The new round was based on the .222 Remington Magnum, which, in turn, had been developed by Remington in conjunction with Springfield Armory. The .223 was created by expanding the case of the .222 Magnum slightly to allow more powder to be used and to keep the more powerful round from being chambered in rifles created for the original round. These first rounds had a 55-grain FMJ bullet.

The U.S. military cartridge with the 55-grain bullet was designated the M193, with a sister tracer round known as the M196. The M193 had a plain copper jacket, while the tracer had an orange tip. A purple-tipped blank cartridge, the M200, was added to fire ballistic grenades, and a dummy round, the M199, was sometimes used in training or when armorers worked on the AR-15 rifles.

The new round proved effective in combat and became popular with target shooters and varminters. The survivalist movement of the 1970s and 1980s, with its demand for combat-style rifles, also increased the popularity of the round.

Because of the variety of uses to which the round is applied, there is now a wide variety of .223 ammunition. In most Kalashnikov rifles chambered for .223, a barrel twist of one turn in twelve inches of barrel is used. This twist works well with lighter bullets in the 45- to 62-grain range; 52- and 53-grain HP (hollow point) bullets achieve peak accuracy in many rifles. For combat use, expanding bullets give the best performance in the .223 Remington, though FMJs fare better with this round than with nearly any other cartridge. The bullet is not overly stabilized, so that the heavier tail end tries to take the lead when the bullet hits an object. This tumbling motion, accompanied by twisting imparted by the barrel's rifling, causes the bullet to create a more massive wound channel that tends to be the length of the bullet rather than its width.

A secondary action also often occurs with cannelured .223 bullets. This bullet fragments into two or more pieces along the weak spot created by the cannelure, with the various parts cutting wound channels that branch from each other. This, coupled with the high speed and tumbling effect, makes the .223 very deadly, even in its FMJ form.

Above 62 grains, .223 bullets have to become fat to remain stable and accurate with the 1-in-12 twist. The trade-off is that they lose much of their ballistic efficiency and suffer a greater velocity decrease than longer bullets would. One example of such a bullet is Speer's 70-grain SSP (Semi-spitzer Soft Point) which is designed for use in 1-in-12 barrels; its less tapered shape allows it to be stabilized by the slower twist.

With faster twists of 1-in-10 or 1-in-7, it would seem that the round's stability would decrease its tumbling effect and make the FMJ versions less likely to be lethal. In fact, the bullets often prove lethal more often since the fragmenting effect is greater due to increased centrifugal pressure of the bullet's jacket. This—and the need for greater long-range accuracy—led to the creation of the 5.56x45mm NATO round.

One caution: bullets designed for varminting have thin metal jackets which allow the projectile to come apart quickly to expend its energy in a small animal. These are not effective combat or large game hunting bullets; they may cause only a superficial wound or even break apart on small obstacles like grass or twigs. With fast twists of 1-in-9 or 1-in-7, the bullets can actually tear apart in the air before coming anywhere near the target. Varminting bullets are often marketed as "SX" (Super eXplosive). If a varmint round is needed and the Kalashnikov has a 1-in-12 twist, Federal's Blitz is an excellent choice; it has a 40-grain bullet which obtains a very high speed that is sudden death for small animals.

Communist-made corrosive ammunition offers good prices at the expense of wear to the rifle and extra cleaning chores. A far better money-saving choice is Winchester's USA ammunition or Federal's American Eagle. Both are loaded to military specifications (for the M193) with a 55-grain FMJ bullet, a reloadable Boxer-primed brass cartridge, and attractively low price tags.

The U.S. military created a plastic practice round with a light metal core for the .223. The lightweight plastic bullet has a high muzzle velocity but quickly sheds velocity so that it can be used for target practice in confined areas. Because of the initial high velocity, it might be used as a self-defense round inside buildings where the overpenetration of an ordinary rifle round would pose dangers to innocent bystanders in other parts of the structure. Unfortunately, these rounds are not readily available in the civilian marketplace.

Since the Kalashnikov action lacks a hold-open device, the use of tracers can show when a magazine has been depleted. A good source of tracer ammunition is Phoenix Systems, Inc.; cost is about $10.95 per pack of ten.

5.56x45mm NATO/M855

In the late 1970s and early 1980s, NATO decided to adopt a new second standard round based on the U.S. .223 Remington. Strangely enough, the new cartridge was originally created by Europeans in an effort to make the .223 less lethal. The idea was to increase the bullet weight and use a faster barrel twist to keep the projectile stable; when a victim was hit, the wound would only be the size of the bullet's diameter, since it wouldn't tumble. The round was promoted by the "humanitarians" who wanted to bring an end to the "barbaric" American bullet, which caused more massive wounds.

The NATO trials came and went and the Belgian SS109 (the U.S. military's M855) design was adopted along with a similar tracer round (the U.S. military's M856). The humanitarians were happy, but many others in the States decried the great mistake the U.S.

military had made because now the "boys in the field" would be strapped with an ineffective round. In fact, the new round has proven to be far more lethal than the FMJ M193. The new rifling created so much tension on the bullet's jacket that it came apart on impact with tissue. The massive wound was not unlike that created by an expanding hunting bullet.

Even though no Kalashnikov rifles chambered for .223 currently have a fast enough twist to fully stabilize the 5.56mm NATO round (a 1-in-9 to 1-in-7 twist is needed rather than the 1-in-12 normally encountered), one will probably be offered either by Valmet or with the Israeli Galil in the near future (the Netherlands' version of the Galil has the 1-in-7 twist, should this supplier make replacement barrels available).

The standard 5.56mm NATO bullet has a hardened steel penetrator embedded inside its tip. This, coupled with the narrow diameter and advanced ballistic coefficient, gives it greater penetration of steel plates, helmets, etc., than the standard .308 Winchester/7.62mm NATO round. While this penetrative ability seems to be at odds with the bullet's ability to fragment, in fact it is not. Steel plates are much thinner than a living target; the bullet can penetrate them before it breaks apart.

If and when the faster twist barrel needed for full stabilization of the 5.56mm NATO round becomes available in .223 Kalashnikovs, it would have great potential wounding effect as a combat rifle (especially for those who must use FMJ ammunition due to the conventions of war or other regulations). Currently, a Yugoslavian-made version of this round with non-corrosive primers is available from the Hansen Cartridge Company and from PMC.

7.62x39mm M43

As noted earlier, the Russian 7.62x39mm M43 was first used in the Simonov SKS56 and later in the AK47. The round proved effective in combat and was slowly adopted by many countries in the Soviet sphere of influence. The round is generally referred to as the M43 in Soviet literature, but it is also known as the M67 in Warsaw Pact countries. These cartridges are nearly identical; the designations are apparently dates of adoption by the Soviets and the Warsaw Pact countries.

The standard M43 cartridge's steel case is brass-plated or lacquered to protect it from rust, with Berdan primers normally being used. Bullet design can vary greatly; the most common type has a steel jacket with a lead sleeve and steel core. The nose of the standard round is unpainted; special-purpose ammunition has paint on its tip.

The 7.62x39mm packs more punch than the .223/5.56mm. Some of its bullets occasionally tumble nearly as soon after impact as the U.S. round, but core inserts of steel and bullet weights from 122 to 150 grains can cause its performance to vary greatly. Most 7.62x39mm FMJ bullets remain stable for the length needed for a bullet to pass through a human being. This means that when FMJ bullets are being used, the 7.62x39mm is slightly inferior to the 7.62mm NATO/.308 Winchester and quite inferior to the 5.56x45mm/.223 Remington and 5.56mm NATO. However, the 7.62x39mm is certainly lethal in its own right: expanding bullets overcome any shortcomings in their wounding potential.

One great drawback with the 7.62x39mm is that its lower speed gives a curved trajectory that makes it impractical for many long-range applications. The round is quite effective within common combat ranges of under 150 yards.

Although most major U.S. companies don't offer the 7.62x39mm cartridge at the time of this writing, this will undoubtedly change in the near future; Federal Cartridge Company leads the industry with the introduction of a new 124-grain FMJ 7.62x39mm round under the "American Eagle" label, with a soft point load slated to be out by the time this book is in print. Unlike most foreign ammunition, the Federal cartridges use Boxer primers, which makes them easy to reload.

A quality foreign-made 7.62x39mm cartridge is offered by Hansen Cartridge Company. Unlike most communist-made ammunition, the Yugoslavian 7.62x39mm is non-corrosive, making for fewer cleaning problems, and Boxer-primed for reloading. Two versions are available, one with a 123-grain FMJ and the other a 125-grain Spitzer suitable for both self-defense and hunting. Hansen also offers a Yugoslavian Berdan-primer blank cartridge.

A number of companies offer Chinese ammunition at very competitive prices but these are currently made with corrosive Berdan primers and steel cases, making them dirty and non-reloadable. This ammunition demands careful cleaning after use even in guns with chromed barrels; accuracy often suffers as well. A shooter should think long and hard before saving a few dollars by using corrosive ammunition.

One exception to this is the Chinese Match ammunition, which is created by carefully weighing the bullets used on standard cartridges. This ammunition is slightly less corrosive than other Chinese cartridges and gives groups that are one to two inches smaller than would be normally expected from a 7.62x39mm Kalashnikov. The ammunition has a boattail FMJ bullet and copper-plated steel cartridge cases. Most Match ammunition has less power than standard cartridges. The Chinese Match ammunition is an exception; it actually has slightly more power. Currently, this ammunition is exported by Poly Tech, with Keng's Firearms being the best source for it in the United States.

For those who do reload this round, care should be taken to purchase Boxer-primed brass cartridges (rather than Berdan) and to try to use lighter .308 bullets so that the bullet velocity is increased and the trajectory stays as flat as possible. Cannelures are a must to prevent the bullet from being forced back into the cartridge during chambering. One good choice is the Speer .308-caliber 130-grain Flat Nose with cannelure. Although the Soviet military loads the 7.62x54R and 7.62x39mm rounds with .310-inch-diameter bullets, the .308 bullets give good results since they seem to swage-fit themselves upon firing.

The 7.62x39mm comes close to the ballistics of the modern .30-30. It would make an excellent short-range deer cartridge which would be legal for hunting in most of the United States with a 5-round magazine.

Military 7.62x39mm ammunition is color coded with lacquer paint on the bullet tips. Unfortunately, this coding varies from country to country. Among the more common military ammunition is the standard "ball" (FMJ); armor piercing (generally with black paint on the bullet tip); incendiary (red paint on tip); grenade launcher blanks (crimped tip); practice blanks (for field exercises with special muzzle attachment); tracers (green paint on nose); short-range practice cartridges (usually with a plastic bullet); and dummy ammunition used for troop training. The most common variation of these rounds is the armor-piercing/incendiary BZ which has a black and red tip; other combinations are also made with two colors of paint being used to denote the bullet's capabilities.

7.62x54mmR

This cartridge was first developed in 1891 as a black powder cartridge with a round-nosed bullet. In 1909, it was modified somewhat with a 150-grain Spitzer bullet. Ballistically, the 7.62x54mmR gives about the same performance as the .308 Winchester or .30-'06 and certainly is not wanting in power. Unfortunately, the rimmed case of this cartridge makes it awkward to use in semi-automatic or automatic weapons, and its power seems to have held back Soviet development of a practical self-loading rifle for decades.

American manufacturers had generally discontinued making the 7.62x54mmR round; until recently it was available in the United States only as an import cartridge from Norma of Sweden, marketed in the States by Federal Cartridge Company. Recently, however, Federal has added the 7.62x54mmR to its American Eagle product line; this cartridge has a 146-grain FMJ-BT bullet and the brass is readily reloadable. Federal also imports the excellent Norma cartridge with a 150-grain soft point bullet.

A wide variety of bullet types is available in most communist countries which use the 7.62x54mmR for their machine guns. Among the most readily available are armor-piercing, tracer, and incendiary bullets as well as combinations of the three. A special load with a low powder charge is also made; it seems to be designed for sniper use with a silencer.

.308 Winchester/7.76mm NATO

The .308 Winchester was developed in the 1950s as an alternative to the .30-'06. The .308 cartridge is shorter than the old round but offers nearly the same punch, thanks to more modern powders. Shortly after the U.S. military adopted the round as the M59, Winchester introduced civilian versions as its .308 Winchester. It was later adopted as the principal NATO rifle round.

Though the new 5.56mm SS109 ammunition comes close to rivaling much of the .308's performance, this changes when expanding or saboted bullets are used. Therefore, while the .308 loaded with FMJ bullets may be inferior to the .223 in wounding effects, it has a lot to offer when other bullets are used with it. Too, even though the .308 doesn't give much extra range over the new 5.56mm SS109, the .308 still bucks crosswinds a bit better, which can be an important consideration in many areas.

The price paid for the .308's pluses include greater expense, increased weight, and greater recoil. Currently, the 150- and 180-grain Spitzer boattail rounds seem best for general use in Kalashnikovs chambered for this round, though this may vary according to the ammunition and firearm. Hunting rounds are also good for combat when the use of expanding bullets isn't banned. Military users may also have access to tracer rounds in this chambering with armor-piercing rounds, like the U.S. M61, occasionally found as well.

In the hunting arena, Federal's Hi-Shok ammunition is very good; these soft-point rounds are available with 150- and 180-grain bullets. Winchester also offers its excellent Silvertip ammunition in both 150- and

180-grain weights. Also notable for accuracy in .308 is Norma ammunition, which is currently being distributed by the Federal Cartridge Company.

One special-purpose bullet found on some .308 rounds is the Glaser Safety Slug. The safety slug uses a copper jacket which surrounds a core of small lead shot pellets rather than a solid lead core. When the bullet hits flesh and blood, it opens up shortly after penetrating the skin; the shot spreads out and cuts a large swath through tissue. The damage isn't a lot greater than that of standard expanding bullets. The real plus comes if innocent bystanders are about in an urban setting; the safety slug tends to break apart and quickly lose energy rather than ricochet dangerously. Unfortunately the Glaser Safety Slug carries a high price tag and is not quite as accurate as more conventional rounds. Nevertheless, it may prove useful for some purposes; Glaser Safety Slugs are available from Phoenix Systems, Inc., for about $23.60 for a pack of six rounds in .308.

Another interesting round in .308 is the West German plastic training round, which has an 11-grain plastic bullet with a high muzzle velocity. The lightweight round quickly sheds velocity so that it can be used in confined areas for target practice. Currently, the round is imported into the United States by Hansen Cartridge Company.

For those concerned with the large groups many Kalashnikovs fire, Federal Cartridge's Match ammunition will often shrink groups by an inch or two. Even though this won't bring most rifles into Western Match standards, it will make them suitable for shooting at longer ranges where greater than normal accuracy is called for.

.50 BMG

Although there is no .50-caliber variation of the Kalashnikov and even though Western machine guns chambered for the .50 BMG (Browning Machine Gun) are quite good, a version of the Kalashnikov may be created with the .50 BMG chambering, since the cartridge is very similar to the Soviet 12.7x108mm. In addition to being a bit more powerful than the Soviet round, a wide variety of ammunition has been created for the .50 BMG over the years.

Olin Corporation produces some exotic rounds in .50 BMG, including the SLAP round, which has a sharp tungsten penetrator encased in a plastic boot. After the bullet leaves the barrel, the plastic sleeve drops away and the penetrator travels on at a high speed capable of defeating the light armor on the Soviet BMP armored personnel carrier. A companion SLAP tracer round is also being produced, since the round has different ballistics than standard .50 BMG ammunition.

Another interesting .50 BMG round is the MP (multi-purpose) round produced in the United States by Olin under license from A/S Raufoss, and by A/S Raufoss in Europe. This cartridge incorporates an incendiary explosive charge in its bullet which is detonated shortly after impact, giving it time to penetrate light armor before igniting. This makes it effective against lightly armored trucks and personnel carriers, airplanes, and helicopters.

More readily available .50 BMG rounds include the U.S. M33 Ball and M17 tracer, as well as several blank and limited-range training rounds. Hansen currently offers ammunition loaded to M33 standards.

Several new trends will spur on the creation of new .50 BMG rounds. One is the use of the round in long-range sniper rifles; such use will require more accurate ammunition as well as better ballistic designs for the bullets. Another change will take place with the creation of a new .50-caliber machine gun to replace the aging Browning machine guns in U.S. arsenals. The replacement weapon is to be gas-operated so that it can handle ammunition of varying powers. Both of these changes promise to inspire new cartridges in this chambering which will make it ideal for use in Kalashnikov spinoff designs.

12.7x108mm

The Soviet 12.7x108mm is only slightly longer than the .50 BMG cartridge; its bullet has the same diameter. Ballistically, it is slightly inferior to the Browning round.

Not a lot is known in the West about the 12.7x108mm round, but it seems probable that, in addition to standard ball, armor-piercing, tracer, and incendiary bullets (as well as combinations of the three) are available. Given the Soviet tendency to borrow Western technology, another possible bullet type would be a saboted round capable of defeating more armor than the standard AP round.

Specifications for Rifle Cartridges

Name	Bullet Weight (gr.)	Overall Length (in.)	Muzzle Velocity (FPS)	Muzzle Energy (FPE)
.22 Short	29	0.676	1,132	83
.22 Long	29	0.880	1,180	90
.22 CB Long Cap	29	0.883	727	33
.22 LR (Standard)	40	0.981	1,138	116
.22 LR (High Vel.)	40	0.981	1,255	140
.22 LR (Hyper Vel.)	32	0.981	1,640	191
.22 Magnum Short	40	0.981	*	*
.22 WMR	40	1.350	1,910	324
5.45x39mm	53	2.22	2,950	1,024
.223 Remington	55	2.25	3,100	1,174
5.56mm NATO	62	2.25	3,100	1,323
7.62x39mm	122	2.20	2,400	1,560
7.62x55mmR	150	3.02	2,800	2,620
.308 Winchester (7.62x51mm NATO)	150	2.75	2,860	2,730
.50 BMG	710	5.42	2,810	12,452
12.7x108mm	681	5.76	2,700	11,026

* Experimental round; exact figures unknown at time of this writing.

Note: Specifications vary greatly from manufacturer to manufacturer and from country to country. The figures shown above are approximate only; for exact figures, the user should check literature supplied by the manufacturer of the specific brand of ammunition in question.

Chapter 7

Accessories
for the Kalashnikov Rifles

A wide array of military accessories is made for the Kalashnikov rifles, augmented by devices created for RPK machine guns. As AKs become more popular in the United States and elsewhere, many more add-ons designed specifically for the rifle will probably appear.

When it comes to accessories, moderation is a virtue. The Kalashnikov is already a heavy weapon; adding much to it in the way of scopes, bayonets, bipods, and slings can quickly turn it into a land anchor. Whether the rifle is used to shoot tin cans and targets or enemy troops, too much gear can be a genuine liability.

Those using a Kalashnikov for actual fighting should take great pains not to get burdened with various types of gear, canned food, extra clothing, bedrolls, and so on. In the Vietnam War, the Vietcong learned that American troops tended to carry too much equipment to move quickly. While the GIs generally won protracted battles thanks to better training and supplies, hit-and-run tactics often killed many of them before they could lumber off a trail and out of the way of stray bullets. When precise shooting is called for or when a person is facing combat, on-person gear should be minimal.

A good rifle, quality ammunition, and five or six reliable magazines are about the only essentials in most cases. Those planning on staying out in the "boonies" will, of course, need more. But, again, care should be taken to limit the burden not to what *might* be needed, but to what can't be done without. My personal choices for extended travel on foot with a Kalashnikov include a good pocket knife with at least one screwdriver blade, a first aid kit with one large GI bandage, a canteen and water purification tablets, maybe a rifle sling, a poncho, a small .22 pistol like the Ruger Mark II or Jennings .22, and a long-bladed combat knife like Sherwood International's SI-5 Eickhart. Everyone has his own needs and skills; some thought should be given to what is needed, especially in areas where shelter or foul weather gear might be needed.

The way gear is carried can also make or break a rifleman; a belt and harness with pouches, a combat vest, or some such arrangement is considered a must, although you can get by with just a belt and trouser pockets. In general, military harnesses and pouches usually aren't called for unless a protracted battle is anticipated; often lightweight commercial pouches and belts like those put out by Uncle Mike's make a lot more sense.

In addition to traveling as light as possible, try gear out with a rifle *before* the rifle is needed. Often, some types of accessories or other gear aren't compatible. Discovering that a sling blocks the ejection port or a scope locked onto the rifle with hex nuts (and no hex wrench available) prevents field stripping can be a disaster. Such an event can even be fatal in battle.

The bane of many shooters' existences are accessories that need a hex driver, L wrench, or special screwdriver to tighten, remove, or adjust them. Those with a Kalashnikov that needs such accessories should either carry the special tool called for and be careful not to lose it, or replace the Phillips-head screws, hex bolts, hex nuts, or whatever with standard slot-headed screws or wing nuts. While it calls for a bit of extra work, it is also possible to cut a screwdriver slot into hex- or Phillips-head screws or bolts with a hacksaw; use a file to get the slot started and then the hacksaw to cut the groove.

Many accessories also shoot loose at the worst of times; the cure for this is a drop of Loctite applied to the threads of the guilty equipment. But care must be taken since Loctite is sometimes forever and a day in coming loose again. Be certain that everything is just right before using this glue.

If a shooter is planning on using a Kalashnikov as a survival or combat weapon, he shouldn't mount fragile gear on it, since this can negate the one big plus of the AKs: their toughness. Some thought should be given as to whether accessories mounted on a rifle will survive a drop. Think about what possible hazards of Mother Nature in the form of rain, snow, dust, sand, and so on may do to high-tech gear. Batteries can be iffy as well; a shooter using electrical gear should have spare batteries at hand in the field.

When a shooter tests equipment, he should be sure it doesn't hamper his movement or slow him down, especially in brush where loops, projections, or even long magazines act like small fingers to stick and snag. Duck-billed flash suppressors, slings, and heavy night-vision equipment are all poor in the brush and better suited for use in a stationary position.

In short, there's a lot of good equipment which can

enhance the use of a Kalashnikov. The trick is to discover which accessories are right and to avoid wasting money on extraneous equipment. That said, let's look at some specific equipment.

Air Rifles

Because of the expense of ammunition and the lack of space in which to shoot even a .22 rifle in many populated areas, many riflemen have found that an air rifle is very useful in perfecting shooting techniques, honing good habits, and keeping in practice. Many air guns have good trigger pulls and demand proper technique in order to hit their marks. The low cost of air gun pellets also encourages a lot of practice.

Chinese AK-style air rifle is imported by Navy Arms Company. This rifle has adjustable sights which give a sight picture identical to that of a Kalashnikov.

There are many modern air rifles on the market; first choice would be the Chinese-made AK-style rifle distributed and sold by Navy Arms Company in the United States. This rifle's sights are nearly identical to the AKM's; both are adjustable and give a sight picture identical to that of a Kalashnikov. The rifle fires standard .177 pellets and is spring powered, with the cocking lever on its right side. The stock is similar to the Soviet

AK74 metal folding stock with a positive lockup. The gun has the feel of an AK thanks to its seven-pound heft; muzzle velocity is in the intermediate range, making it good for clearing out pests at close ranges. Navy Arms offers the rifle for about $79, considerably less than most air rifles in its class.

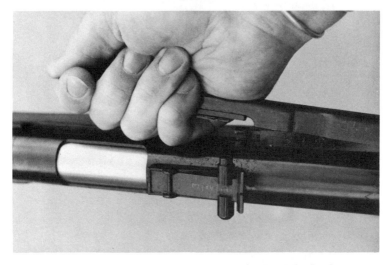

The Navy Arms Chinese air rifle is cocked with the lever on the right side of the gun's receiver. Note the adjustable rear sight.

Another air rifle of interest is Daisy's Powerline 814. Although modeled after the Mini-14 rifle, the single-pump pneumatic's pistol grip gives it a feel similar to many Kalashnikovs. The rear sight is a peep sight (the front is a ramp blade) so that the sight picture is not like that of most Kalashnikovs, however, and the rifle is considerably lighter. But as an inexpensive practice rifle for honing instinctive shooting skills or for those with a rear peep sight version of the Kalashnikov, this rifle might be just the ticket. The Powerline 814 is available at many discount stores at a very reasonable price.

Since the rifle can shoot BBs from its integral magazine as well as .177 pellets fed into it by hand, it is quick to reload and very inexpensive to use.

Folding stock on Navy Arms' Chinese air rifle. Note AR-15-style safety.

Bayonets

Anyone who has read my other books knows that I'm not going to recommend mounting a bayonet on a rifle. They are mean looking and no doubt add a lot to military parades around the world, but they are useless in modern combat with a large-magazine, dependable rifle like the Kalashnikov.

Bayonets haven't seen use in hand-to-hand combat since before the Korean War and, even then, such combat was very limited. As most any GI who served in Vietnam can tell you, and as Brigadier General S.L.A. Marshall wrote in the May/June 1967 issue of *Infantry,* the bayonet was never used for fighting on the end of a rifle in Vietnam.

Most Kalashnikov bayonets mounted on a rifle don't work for more than one stab. The reason? The blade is so wide on nearly all Soviet and Warsaw Pact bayonets that the friction it creates, coupled with the force of a two-handed jab, almost always makes it impossible to pull the bayonet out of an impaled foe. The only exception to this is the spike bayonet, which has low enough friction to make it possible to withdraw the blade from a wounded foe. But even with a spike bayonet, all is not well. The overall package of the rifle and bayonet is too long and awkward for use in most close-combat situations.

Consequently, troops in combat use empty rifles as clubs when nothing else is available, or entrenching tools and hunting knives when time permits. All are better hand-to-hand combat weapons than the bayonet.

There are exceptional cases, such as parades and guarding prisoners, in which the Soviet-style blade looks nice. The spike bayonet is ideal for handling prisoners in case several have to be engaged, since it can be pulled from a human body without getting hopelessly caught.

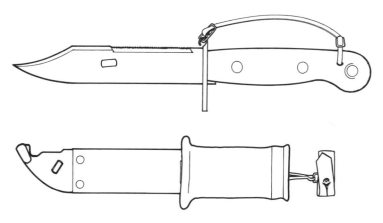

Soviet-style bayonets (like this one available from Rhino for about $25) make good fighting knives. The bayonet and scabbard can also be used as a makeshift wire cutter. [Drawing courtesy of Rhino Replacement Parts.]

Soviet-style bayonets make good fighting knives and are relatively inexpensive (though some Soviet bayonets have such a high temper that they're hard to sharpen). Many Soviet-style bayonets also have a rectangular cutout in the blade which acts as a pivot point for a small tab in the bayonet scabbard. Together, the bayonet and scabbard can then be used as a makeshift wire cutter. This could be a plus once in a great while, though the hassle of getting the scabbard off the belt and assembling the two could be quite a problem—especially in the dark. One slip can cause a nasty cut since the bayonet has a sharp exposed blade when used as a wire cutter.

Bayonets, even with the wire cutter option, are more gimmicky than useful. A shooter should save his money unless he wants to use a bayonet as a knife.

Bipods

Like the bayonet, bipods are nearly useless in many types of combat except for defending a fixed position. They can be of use in target shooting or varminting and look nifty when a rifle is displayed on a table at a gun show, but out in the wilds most bipods are too short to allow a shooter to see what he's shooting at. Unless the Kalashnikov is a sniping or SAW variant (which generally have their own bipods) and will be used in a fixed position where fields of fire can be cleared, a shooter is wise not to plan on using a bipod.

There are several clothespin-style bipods which clip onto the Kalashnikov's barrel. The military bipod designed for the AR-15 will work, though it is rather rust-prone in wet or humid conditions.

One of the best clothespin bipods is offered by Ram-Line. Its nylon bipod works the same way as the military model, but fits almost any diameter barrel and is less apt to mar the firearm's finish; it comes with a plastic locking device which allows it to be carried closed. The Ram-Line bipod costs about $15.

Brass Catchers

E&L Manufacturing makes a good rigid brass catcher for the Kalashnikovs for around $25; its Brass Catcher (what else could they name it?) works well and can save reloaders a lot of time and money. While these catchers work without a hitch, it is still wise to avoid using them in a survival or combat situation; better to waste brass than take even a very minor chance of jamming the rifle.

A brass catcher is a must for reloaders since it keeps the shooter from developing the habit of trying to watch where brass goes following a shot, a habit that has actually gotten some policemen using semiauto weapons killed when they finally fired shots in combat.

Camouflage

While camouflage doesn't guarantee that a shooter won't be seen (movement or standing in the open will quickly defeat the best of camo patterns), it can greatly improve his chances of success at his shooting endeavors; and it can save his life in combat.

Many otherwise well-camouflaged shooters can be spotted by their uncamouflaged gun. The best and easiest way to camouflage a weapon is to paint it in a pattern that matches the environment in which it will be used. Take care to plug the barrel and cover moving parts so the firearm won't get gummed up by the paint. It's also wise to clean the surface of the rifle with acetone beforehand to remove any grease or oil that will keep paint from sticking.

Flat (not glossy) spray paint works well; the prudent will practice their camo paint techniques on cardboard before tackling a good rifle. The dominant color of the camouflage pattern should be applied first. After the paint has dried, paper stencils are taped to the rifle or, for quick and dirty work, vegetation is laid over parts of the rifle and another color added. Once that's dried, the first layer of stencils (or leaves and weeds) is left in place and another added; then the final color of paint is sprayed on. When the third coat has dried, the two layers of stencils are removed, and the rifle camouflage is complete.

Brigade Quartermasters offers a good camo spray paint set of four colors (brown, olive drab, black, and tan) for about $17 for the set.

For temperate areas where both snow and warm weather are expected, a white cloth cover to go over the green/black/brown summer camouflage of the rifle makes for a quick change. Since cold weather is less apt to create overheating problems, it's possible to get away with covering the barrel this way. Care should be taken not to block the ejection port, sights, trigger, selector, or magazine well with any material, however.

Camo tape designed for hunters is also ideal for those who may need several types of camouflage as the surroundings change. Brigade Quartermasters carries three styles of camo tape (green, brown, and gray) for around $6 per roll; one roll will cover one gun.

Carrying Cases

A carrying case is quite useful to store a Kalashnikov or to transport it in when traveling. A case also allows you to carry the rifle through a populated area without raising a panic.

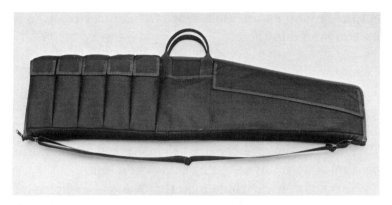

First choice in carrying cases for AKs is Uncle Mike's Assault Rifle Case. The case also can carry magazines and a bipod, bayonet, or what have you. [Photo courtesy of Michaels of Oregon.]

Many good soft cases are available. First choice is Uncle Mike's Assault Rifle Case, which is readily available in gun stores and which fits the Kalashnikov perfectly. The case has five flapped magazine pouches and a long accessory pouch for bipod, bayonet, or what have you; all are secured by Velcro closures. The center rifle pocket has a self-healing zipper and the entire case is made of tough padded cordura nylon to protect the rifle. A removable shoulder strap can be mounted on the case and two handy carrying handles are sewn into the top. Retail cost is about $59.

If a carrying case is only needed occasionally, a less expensive one may make more sense. Though they are less durable and offer less protection to the rifle, a heavy canvas case with a lint-free, corduroy lining is often satisfactory for limited use. These are available for around $28 each in black, olive green, or camo from Parellex or Sherwood International.

Don't purchase a carrying case made of vinyl or other non-breathing plastic; these allow moisture to collect inside and can cause major rust and corrosion to a firearm stored in them.

Cartridge Adapters

Unlike many other military rifles, semiauto .22 conversion kits are not available for Kalashnikovs. Most shooters will find, however, that cartridge adapters or .22 rifles modeled after the Kalashnikovs will fulfill most roles normally taken by conversion kits.

Harry Owen cartridge adapters are one inexpensive way to fire .22s or other rounds from Kalashnikovs one shot at a time. The cartridge adapters are a bit awkward to use since they have to be chambered by hand and require a little work to reload. They are useful for a quick single shot when hunting small game or the like.

Currently, the adapters are readily available for use in rifles chambered for 5.56mm NATO/.223 Remington or 7.62mm NATO/.308 Winchester; 7.62x39mm adapters will probably soon be available in the United States as the Kalashnikovs become more popular.

Harry Owen conversion cartridges are made of brass or steel and look like empty cartridges. Internally, the dimensions of the unit allow a smaller cartridge to be placed inside the adapter and a striker to be placed behind it. When the adapter is chambered, the rifle's firing pin hits the striker, which transfers the energy of the firing pin to the .22's rim to fire it. The cartridge adapter then has to be carefully extracted so that it can be caught rather than ejected and a small rod used to push the striker and spent casing out of the adapter. This done, a new .22 round is dropped into the adapter and the striker pushed into place; the adapter is rechambered in the rifle by pulling back the bolt and holding it in place with one hand while carefully dropping the adapter into the chamber with the other hand. Needless to say, reloading is slow and a quick second shot is not possible, even if the shooter has two adapters to alternate.

The .22 LR adapters can fire .22 LR (standard or high velocity), .22 Long, .22 Short, .22 shot cartridges, and .22 CB Long Caps. Adapters which allow the use of the .22 Magnum family of cartridges are also available. Both the .22 LR and Magnum bullets are close enough in size to the .223 Remington bullet to allow good accuracy. Cost for these adapters is around $19 each for the brass model or about $27 for the steel version.

For Kalashnikovs chambered in .308, similar adapters are also available. Those designed for use with the .22 cartridges have a small barrel built into them, since the .308 caliber is too large to stabilize the spin of a .22 or give it any velocity. Like the .223 adapter, the .308 version allows the use of a wide range of .22 rimfire cartridges; due to the larger bore, adapters are also available for use with .30-caliber cartridges like the .30 Carbine. The .22 adapters cost about $35 each while those for .30-caliber cartridges (which don't need the rifled section), cost about $19 for brass models or about $27 for steel versions.

Harry Owen also offers an adapter which allows .22-caliber air rifle pellets to be fired with a rifle primer which is placed at the end of the unit. These make little noise and propel the pellets fast enough for target shooting. This unit, along with a depriming rod, is available for approximately $24.

It is also possible to create squib loads which have the low energy and velocity needed for quiet practice, or hunting small game with a Kalashnikov. Besides being less expensive to shoot, squib loads can be cycled through the magazine of the rifle without the shooter having to chamber each one by hand, as is the case with cartridge adapters. Various types of squib—as well as lead plinker—loads for both the .223 and .308 are outlined in *Combat Ammunition,* available from Paladin Press. Unfortunately, at the time of this writing, the author and others haven't had time to work up good squib loads.

Eye Protection

The Kalashnikov design doesn't give as much protection to a shooter as does a rifle with a milled receiver should a round fire prematurely, the bolt fail to lock up when a round is fired, or some other mishap occur. In such a case, the sheet-metal receiver cover is apt to be blown off the rifle; this flying piece of metal can easily strike the shooter's face. Wearing protective glasses would greatly minimize the injury such an accident could cause.

In battle, many eye injuries result from secondary projectiles such as rock chips, sand, or bullet fragments. Again, proper eye protection enables a shooter to continue fighting.

Hunters aren't exempt from shooting accidents; more than a few have been blinded by stray shotgun pellets or long-range shots made without a proper backstop.

Fortunately, modern polycarbonate sunglasses are available. While they cannot stop high-speed projectiles like rifle bullets or even many pistol bullets, they can stop most secondary missiles like bullet fragments and rock chips. They can also stop small shot pellets as well as air rifle and many .22 bullets.

Several good sunglasses and clear goggles made of polycarbonate are offered by Jones Optical Company. Another popular polycarbonate sunglass is the Gargoyle offered by Brigade Quartermasters.

Flash Hiders and Muzzle Brakes

Most Western assault rifles have flash hiders, muzzle brakes, or combinations of the two. Flash hiders or flash suppressors (which are not the same as silencers or sound suppressors) do away with much of the muzzle flash created by unburnt powder. Though not needed in the daytime, when sunlight makes muzzle flash unnoticeable, a flash hider is a must for nighttime combat.

A muzzle brake takes some of the energy of the gas near the muzzle and rechannels it so that the jet propels the barrel counter to the recoil of the rifle (i.e., forward and to the side) to reduce muzzle climb and felt recoil. The trade-off for this action is often increased muzzle flash and noise, though a few Western brakes have been successfully combined with flash hiders.

Muzzle brakes are ideal for automatic fire, especially with more powerful cartridges like the .308 Winchester and 7.62x54mmR. Even in semiauto fire with cartridges like the .223, a muzzle brake can make follow-up shots considerably quicker.

The Galil and Valmet rifles both have excellent flash hiders. So do most communist sniper weapons and machine guns. But, although communist doctrine stresses night fighting, their rifles almost never have flash hiders; and, except for the muzzle brake on the AK74, most communist-made Kalashnikov infantry rifles have only rudimentary muzzle brakes, which are simply a muzzle extension nut with the end cut at an angle.

A number of companies make flash suppressors. A muzzle compensator based on the Soviet AK74 is also available for use on all AKs. Made in the United States, the compensator costs about $33.50 and is available from Rhino Replacement Parts, Inc. In addition to pushing the barrel down and to the side to compensate for the recoil of the weapon, it also acts like a muzzle brake and reduces felt recoil. Like the Soviet muzzle brake, this version creates a lot of muzzle noise and the blowing of gas to each side of the muzzle can be a problem to shooters to either side; it can also raise a cloud of dust during prone shooting.

Rhino Replacement Parts also offers an AKSU-Krinkov flash hider for about $20, which is reverse-threaded to fit models of 7.62x39mm and .223 Chinese and Russian AKs. Mitchell Arms, Inc., imports AR-15-style flash hiders from Yugoslavia. These bird cage flash hiders were apparently designed for use on RPKs but are readily mounted on most communist-made AKs. The cost is about $39.

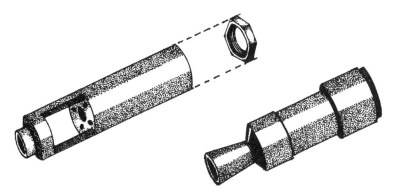

American-made AK74-style muzzle brakes (left) and AKSU Krinkov-style flash hider/muzzle brakes (right) are available from Rhino Replacement Parts to fit most communist-made AKs in 7.62x39 and .223. [Drawing courtesy of Rhino Replacement Parts.]

Perhaps the best compensator is the DTA Mil/Brake (formerly the Muzzle Mizer) from Fabian Brothers Sporting Goods for around $36. The real plus of the DTA Mil/Brake is that it reduces flash considerably, reduces actual recoil by up to 45 percent (with the .223 version), and reduces muzzle flip as well. It is adjustable for left- or right-handed shooters.

The DTA Mil/Brake is available for the AKM/ AK47S/AK47 Chinese and most communist-made semiauto and selective-fire versions of the Kalashnikov in 7.62x39mm; a separate model of the brake is also available for .223/5.56 chamberings. Another slightly different DTA Mil/Brake is available for the Galil rifles, with different-sized brakes for the .308 and .223 models. The price of the DTA Mil/Brake is about $35 each; each unit screws onto the barrel threads on the rifle's muzzle.

Grenade Launchers

As far back as World War I, a number of countries created grenades which could be fired from rifles; a few countries still produce such grenades for use with Kalashnikovs. This method of launching grenades requires the use of a blank cartridge. Too, the grenades' accuracy is less than perfect, since sighting systems were almost impossible to use and many guns didn't have any grenade sights. The grenades must be small, or the power of the blank needed to fire a large grenade will soon wreck the gun with abusive recoil.

Another solution to the problem of launching grenades is to use a launcher attached to a rifle. This creates a sort of portable one-man mortar while not depriving the user of a way to defend himself. Perhaps the best known of these launchers is the US M203 which consists of an AR-15 (M16) rifle with a grenade launcher mounted below its barrel. Following the successful deployment of this weapon in Vietnam, other countries have created their own versions.

One copycat version of the M203 is believed to have been developed by the Soviet Union as a 40mm grenade launcher mounted under the new AK74 assault rifle. Little is known about the weapon at the time of this writing.

A U.S.-based company, J.C. Manufacturing, Inc., has recently introduced a modified version of the M203 which it calls the M203 PI (Product Improved). The launcher has a universal mounting system so that it can be placed on a number of rifles, including the Galil, AK47, AKM, and most Kalashnikov variants.

The J.C. Manufacturing mounting system allows the M203 PI launcher to be quickly mounted or removed from the rifle. Additionally, the new PI version has a longer breech opening so that new, longer grenade rounds can be used with it.

In an effort to break into the law-enforcement market, J.C. Manufacturing also makes 12-gauge, 37mm, and 38mm versions of the M203 PI, so that the launchers can be used with shotgun ammunition, training ammunition, or tear gas grenades.

Hearing Protection

These days, a shooter doesn't need to lose some or all of his hearing to muzzle blast. While hearing protection isn't practical in combat, those who use it in practice often have the edge over those who don't; sometimes, hearing a sound clearly will decide whether a combatant locates a foe or becomes his enemy's victim.

To maintain your hearing, it's important to use hearing protectors even when practicing with a short-barreled .22 rifle, and especially in indoor ranges. Over time, the noise can take its toll on hearing; a centerfire rifle can do measurable damage with just a few rounds when proper hearing protection isn't used.

Another plus of hearing protection is that it helps to prevent the development of a flinch; this in itself makes hearing protectors a worthwhile investment.

Earmuffs designed to give maximum ear protection are most ideal. But if earmuffs aren't available, even expanding, disposable plastic plugs give a lot of protection for very little money.

Laser Sights

Lasers create coherent beams of intense light which travel over long distances without spreading out. Recently, a number of lasers have been marketed which are small and tough enough to be mounted on a rifle and used as aiming devices.

Using one of these is simple. The laser is mounted on a scope-style mount and its beam adjusted so it strikes at the same point as the rifle's bullet at 100 yards. The rifle is fired when the dot of light created by the laser is on target. The bullet strikes within inches of the dot of light out to 300 yards.

The discrepancy of several inches between points of aim and impact at longer ranges occurs because the bullet follows a ballistic arc while the beam of laser light is perfectly straight. Such errors aren't of much concern in hunting or combat, especially given the large groups fired by most Kalashnikovs. Even this small aiming error can be compensated for, since the radius of the laser beam spreads very slowly from its dime-sized spot until it is several feet wide several hundred yards away. A shooter can use the lower edge of the laser beam as an aiming point to compensate for bullet drop, all without even shouldering the rifle or looking through a conventional sight. Lasers do have their drawbacks, however. They can generally be seen by the target as well as people on either side of the user. This creates few problems in hunting but is a concern in combat, where the laser should only be turned on a moment before firing. Positions can also be given away when the laser beam becomes visible in fog or smoke or is seen in night-vision equipment; great care must be exercised in using a laser in combat. Infrared lasers which produce a beam invisible to the naked eye are also available. The shooter wears special night-vision goggles to see the laser's spot and aims in the same manner as when using a visible laser. The catch is the expense: the laser and night-vision goggles can cost thousands of dollars.

Another major drawback to laser use is the fact that a laser dot is virtually invisible in bright sunlight. This limits its use to indoors or outdoors during twilight or night.

Recently, a number of companies have introduced small lasers that have price tags of only $250 to $500. Among the best is the Lasersight LS 45, which is manufactured in England and distributed in the United States by Avin Industries. These little units are easily mounted on Weaver-type scope bases.

Lasers aren't a cure for poor shooting habits, but do offer convenience and quick aimed fire in dark environments. As such, they are ideal for some situations.

Magazines

One of the most important parts of the Kalashnikov is its magazine; not even this rifle's robust design can overcome the failure of that component. A shooter should never skimp when it comes to purchasing a quality magazine or fail to keep the magazine clean. Magazines wear out and become damaged; when this happens, the shooter should discard them.

New magazines often have sharp edges on the lip that the rounds travel over. While the Kalashnikov bolt carrier is heavy enough to overcome this bit of extra friction, rounding off the sharp lip with a small file or sharp steel blade will eliminate the chance of problems.

A wide range of magazines is available for the Kalashnikovs. The greatest diversity is found in the Chinese 7.62x39mm rifles with 5-, 20-, 30-, and 40-round magazines available as well as a 75-round drum and occasionally a 40-round drum. The .223 versions of the Chinese rifle don't currently have as wide an array of magazines but do have a 99-round drum. Some 5-round magazines available for the AKs are simply 20- or 30-round magazines with a spacer to limit the number of shells that can be inserted. A genuine 5-round magazine is made by Poly Technologies, however, and is available from Keng's and others.

Most countries outside China use 30-round magazines for .223/5.56mm NATO, 5.56x39mm, and 7.62x 39mm chamberings, while 20-round magazines are used in the .308/7.62mm NATO chambering. There are exceptions to this, however, with 40-round magazines being made for the 5.56mm and 7.62x39mm cartridges. Israel has split the difference between the 30- and 40-round magazines with a 35-round standard magazine; a 50-round magazine is available as well.

Most countries that use an RPK-style machine gun also make large-capacity drums which can be used in a Kalashnikov. These are best used for prone shooting since extended magazines tend to "high center" or cause discomfort when the rifleman is forced to prop himself up in a higher-than-normal position.

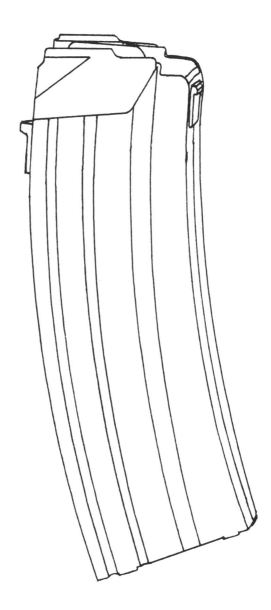

A wide range of Kalashnikov magazines are available. Shown here is a 30-round .223 magazine available from Rhino Replacement Parts as well as other companies. [Drawing courtesy of Rhino Replacement Parts.]

Changing magazines can be a hassle, especially in combat. A number of ways have been developed to couple magazines together to avoid having to fish a full magazine out of a pouch or pocket. The most common, and the worst, way is to use tape to connect magazines together so that the lips of one are up while the other's are down. If the shooter ever has to fire prone or bumps the magazine against something, he's apt to discover it has become full of dirt or the lips are bent. Even the super-reliable Kalashnikov will choke on such a magazine.

A better solution is to use a magazine connector. A.R.M.S. markets excellent connectors as the Mag-Pac system. There are several different models; one is designed for use with all 7.62x39mm Kalashnikov magazines while others are available for the Galil and Valmet rifles in .223 and .308. The Mag-Pac consists of two metal plates separated by a plastic spacer; the plates are bolted together on either side of two magazines so that one magazine sits alongside the other. Magazines can be exchanged by pulling the empty magazine out of the well, and moving the full one into place and rocking it into the well.

Stripper clips are often available for Kalashnikov rifles; these are usually 10-round SKS45 clips. A special loader is needed to transfer rounds from the clip into the magazine. The clips can be of great use when it comes time to recharge a magazine since, with the proper loader, rounds can quickly be chucked into an empty magazine from the clips. Clips should *not* be substituted for loaded magazines in a combat situation; dirt or the "combat shakes" can make them far too slow to use when loaded magazines are desperately needed.

Magazine pouches can accommodate a variety of

magazine sizes and various shooters' needs. China exports canvas bags for RPK drum magazines as well as chest pouches for magazines of varying length; the chest pouch works well but many shooters find it less than comfortable, especially for prone shooting.

Pouches which can be carried on a belt and arranged according to the shooter's wishes are much more practical than chest pouches. One interesting variant is the Soviet-style issue pouch, made by the Chinese as well as the Russians. It is designed to carry four 30-round magazines along with a cleaning kit or other equipment. This pouch has heavy web belt loops on its back and a carrying strap to help keep the shooter's pants from sagging when the pouch is full. The whole thing can also be supported with just the strap over the shoulder.

A number of magazine pouches are available for use with the AK. Shown here is a European-made, heavy canvas pouch which holds 4 magazines. Cost is about $16 from Rhino Replacement Parts. [Drawing courtesy of Rhino Replacement Parts.]

One drawback to most of these pouches is the use of a small buckle to secure the flap; this is slow to impossible to operate, especially with gloves, and seems like a rather poor design for military use. Visit the sewing section of a local department store and purchase some Velcro strips or snaps to replace the pouch's buckles.

For those using 20- or 30-round .223 magazines, Uncle Mike's new double-magazine belt pouches are good bets. They lie flat against the belt so they don't get snagged on brush or doorways, and they're made of tough nylon so they don't show wear with heavy use the way canvas pouches do. Too, they are available in either camo or black finishes rather than the basic olive green of most other pouches. The Uncle Mike's pouches each hold two magazines and are available at most gunshops for around $14 to $15.

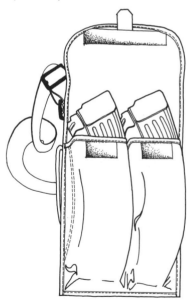

Canvas pouch designed to carry two AK magazines on a belt or with the detachable strap that comes with the pouch. [Drawing courtesy of Rhino Replacement Parts.]

Another possible choice for 30-round .223 magazines is the standard U.S. magazine pouch readily available from Sierra Supply, Sherwood International, and Parellex. Those using .308 rifles with 20-round magazines will find that the U.S. military's M14 pouch is ideal for use with Kalashnikov magazines.

Night Sights

Sights with glow-in-the-dark elements can be of great help in locating a target at night. Unfortunately, they don't work as well as one might suppose, since muzzle flash can ruin a shooter's night vision, making the sights invisible until the eyes readjust to the darkness. Too, if it's so dark that iron sights can't be easily seen, the target is also in the dark; only the glowing sights show up. Thus, while it is possible to see where the rifle is being fired, it may not be possible to tell at what. Nevertheless, Kalashnikovs which have tritium sights or the like have a definite advantage over those that don't.

In order to get used to finding night sights quickly, a rifleman should practice looking at a target in the daylight, and then—with his eyes closed—bring up his weapon and imagine sighting on the target. By opening his eyes when he thinks the rifle is in place, he can quickly see if his rifle is lined up by using the iron sights. After a while, it's possible to acquire the habit of quickly getting a rifle on target by reflex in very dim light. Once close to the target, it's then easy to locate the night sights and use them to full advantage.

Night-Vision Scopes

Night-vision equipment is expensive and heavy—but *very* effective, especially when used to snipe from a fixed position.

There are two types of night-vision scopes: active and passive. The active type sends out a beam of infrared light which is reflected back and processed into visible light on the scope's screen. Because the beam of infrared light is readily seen by other active scope users and looks like a spotlight to those using passive night-vision scopes, active systems are best avoided by those who may face other users of night-vision equipment.

The big plus of active systems is that they're less expensive than other night-vision gear; about the only military users of this type of equipment are Third World countries and the USSR, which is quickly phasing its out. Cost runs from $5,000 to $10,000 for a new active system.

Passive units are similar to TV cameras and boost available light to the point where "what's out there" can be seen on a miniature greenish screen at the scope's rear. Passive scopes need a little light to work, but not much. They do fine with moonlight, starlight, or city glow. Their big plus is that they're smaller than active units and can't be readily spotted by other night-vision users.

First-generation scopes work well where an occasional bright light isn't present to cause streaking and blooming on the scope's screen, which can be a bother or can even shut the screen down for a few critical seconds. First-generation scopes carry lower price tags, however, so they're still being made and sold. Second-generation passive scopes are smaller and can deal with lights, flares, etc., without streaking. A third-generation scope is said to be on the way but is not currently available. Cost of passive scopes runs from $2,000 to $15,000 per unit.

Most scopes need special mounting systems before they can be used with a rifle and must be carefully zeroed—a task not all that easy, given that sunlight can damage most of these scopes. The batteries of both active and passive systems need to be recharged or replaced with alarming regularity and are easily damaged, which makes them better for occasional use in fixed areas rather than for patrols or the like.

Several good companies market night-vision equipment, including Excalibur Enterprises, Litton (Electron Tube Division), and Standard Equipment Co.

Rear Sights

Except for the Galil and some of the Valmet rifles, Kalashnikovs generally have rear sights with a notch rather than the quicker military peep sight. While shooters used to hunting rifles may find this sight to their liking, it is considerably slower to use than the peep sight and also isn't forgiving of older eyes which often have trouble focusing on the notch as well as the target.

It is hoped that some enterprising manufacturer will offer a replacement peep sight for the Kalashnikovs. Until then, the shooter needing such a sight will have to have it custom-made by a local gunsmith. Such work is not overly expensive.

Scopes and Mounts

For many, a scope won't be needed on the Kalashnikov since the rifle is generally used for snap shooting, is already heavy, and isn't noted for great accuracy. At the same time, the Kalashnikov is as accurate as many hunting rifles. For those who dislike using iron sights, a good scope can shorten the time it takes to get the rifle on target.

Scopes are getting better and tougher but don't stand up the way an AK will. Therefore, a scope mounted on this rifle becomes the weak link. Great care should be taken not to drop a scoped Kalashnikov.

The metal receiver cover on the Kalashnikov rifle makes mounting a scope a bit of an engineering nightmare. The best solution seems to be mounts like those created for the Galil and Valmet rifles which anchor the device to the lower receiver and float the scope over the receiver cover. A good Galil-style mount is offered by Rhino Replacement Parts, Inc., for AKs imported into the United States. The unit attaches to the left side of the rifle and allows mounting standard 1-inch Weaver ring mounts to hold a 1-inch rifle scope in place. The cost is about $24.50.

B-Square's old-style scope mount was similar to that of the Galil. While not as quick as their newer scope mount, it did allow the use of standard rifle scopes on AKs. [Photo courtesy of B-Square.]

For a time, B-Square offered a scope mount similar to that used for the Galil. Recently, however, B-Square has come out with one mount that replaces the rear sight of the rifle and another which fastens to the fore grip/gas tube. Both use a pistol scope; standard optical scopes cannot be used with either system, since the eye relief isn't long enough.

B-Square's newest no-gunsmithing scope for the Kalashnikov attaches to the gun's upper handguard and gas tube. One plus is that the gun's iron sights can still be used with the scope in place. [Photo courtesy of B-Square Company.]

While it would seem that these new B-Square scope mounts aren't much of an alternative, they in fact work quite well. The scope blocks less of the shooter's viewing area so that a target can be acquired very quickly; with a "dot" scope like the Armson OEG (Occluded Eye Scope) or Aimpoint, target acquisition is extremely quick. A little practice makes aimed fire nearly as fast as shooting from the hip — only hits are considerably better with aimed fire. Another plus of the B-Square mounts is that they require no gunsmith work and come with good, step-by-step instructions for quick mounting. The cost is around $40 each.

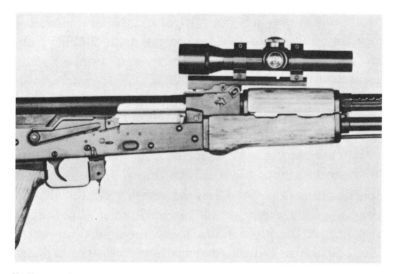

B-Square's new scope mount replaces the rear sight of the Kalashnikov. Using a pistol scope, this setup gives a very quick sight picture, making it possible to rapidly engage moving targets [Photo courtesy of B-Square.]

For those using the Galil or Valmet rifles with factory scope mounts, a wider range of choices is available; nearly any hunting scope can give good results. While range-finding scopes and other variable scopes are not generally warranted on the flat-shooting .223, they might be of use with the .308 or 7.62x39mm.

If the rifle is used in rough-and-tumble conditions, the fixed scope is tougher and is generally a better bet. Too, most of the purchase price for a fixed scope goes toward optics rather than gear work. The 4X is the most versatile and is suited to most hunting as well as combat.

Scopes made by Bausch & Lomb, Beeman (whose lenses are made by the Nikon camera company), Burris, Bushnell, Leupold, Redfield, Shepherd, Swarovski Optik, Simmons, Tasco, Weatherby, and Williams are all pretty good bets. Shooters should *avoid* unknown "bargain" scopes; they are not always reliable and seldom a good buy. When possible, get scopes with the new rubber armor coat or brushed finishes to minimize the chances of reflecting the sunlight.

For those wanting a top-of-the-line scope, the Trijicon series of scopes from Armson offers excellent light-gathering qualities as well as a reticle with a tritium element that glows in the dark, making shooting on moonlit nights practical in many situations. The Spectrum version of the Trijicon series gives the shooter a choice of red, green, or amber reticle color at night and also allows the cross hairs to be daylight-illuminated when firing at a dark target where the normal black cross hairs may be hard to see. Optional rubber eyepieces are available for all models of the scopes to help minimize the effects of light to the side of the shooter's eyes.

For either the B-Square or the Galil/Valmet mounts, dot scopes (which place a dot of light in the field of view rather than in the cross hairs) are quicker to use. Their only drawback is that they don't magnify the target; this can also translate into a plus, since it is quite easy to use the scopes with both eyes open.

One style of dot scope actually requires that both eyes remain open when using it; this is the OEG. Looking through the scope shows a red dot without any view of the target. The view of the target is provided by the shooter's other eye. With both eyes open, the user's brain combines the images to superimpose the dot over the target.

This scope can be confusing at first, since most shooters close one eye when aiming, but once the shooter gets used to the occluded eye system, it is very quick and gives a wide field of view. The occluded eye system can't be used by all shooters; people with vision problems may find that the dot appears to wander about the target. Likewise, those with good vision in only one eye can't use the occluded system.

The best available-light occluded eye scope is the Armson OEG, which costs about $220. The OEG's glow-red dot is easy to find and quick to use in combat shooting *provided* the shooter has practiced enough to be familiar with it. The Armson OEG is also available with a tritium element so that the scope produces a white dot when used in the dark.

A number of dot scopes are also available which create an electronic dot that is superimposed in the shooter's view through the scope; these are not OEGs and can be used with one eye. The catch is that the batteries need replacement from time to time. Unlike the Armson OEG, which adjusts its brightness by the amount of available light, the electric dot scopes have to be adjusted manually to make the dot match the light conditions of the environment. This can be a problem during a partly cloudy day or when moving through heavily wooded areas where the amount of light may vary, but it is a plus when shooting from a dark area into a brightly lit one.

Electric dot scopes can be readily used at night, but don't work as well as might be expected, since night vision is best from the sides of the eye rather than the center.

First choice of the electric dot scopes is Aimpoint's new 2000 series which can be mounted in standard 1-inch rings. The cost is in the neighborhood of $180.

Sight Adjustment Tool

While not essential by any means, the communist-designed tool for quickly adjusting the windage and elevation of a Chinese Kalashnikov (as well as most other AKs) may be of interest. It is available from Keng's Firearms for approximately $35.

Silencers

Silencers (also called sound suppressors) with .22 training versions of the Kalashnikov can quiet the rifles down to a gentle pop. With regular centerfire bullets, however, a loud supersonic crack still occurs which is about as noisy as the normal muzzle blast. For those under fire, however, the lack of muzzle blast makes the shooter very hard to locate even though each shot is readily heard.

There is a number of excellent books on silencers; anyone interested in purchasing a silencer should read up on the device before buying or going through the red tape and $200 purchase tax.

One of the best overview books on the subject is J. David Truby's *Silencers in the 1980s* available from Paladin Press. Truby gives a realistic look at silencer capabilities and types, as well as providing the names and addresses of the major manufacturers. Probably the best-known source of silencers in the United States is Jonathan Arthur Ciener, Inc., which will also do custom modifications of firearms for silencer use.

Slings

There is a wide range of slings available for Kalashnikovs; most military and commercial slings can be readily adapted. Often slings aren't needed—or may even be a hindrance—in combat or while hunting. Some thought should be given before spending a lot of money on one.

The best and some of the most reasonably priced slings are made by Uncle Mike's; models vary from the basket-weave leather Cobra Strap to inexpensive nylon slings in camouflage, brown, black, and white (for use in snow). Slings by Uncle Mike's are very weather resistant and are available in either padded "shoulder savers" or regular straps. Uncle Mike's slings can be found in most gunshops.

Spare Parts Kits

Kalashnikovs are robust enough that companies trying to make money selling spare parts kits could face some very lean days indeed. However, parts are occasionally lost or damaged by abuse or accident. While a good gunsmith could repair or duplicate almost any part in a Kalashnikov without access to factory-made components, the best route would be to order parts from one of the major importers listed in the appendix of this book. Gun Parts will probably stock Kalashnikov parts in the near future; they have done so with nearly every other military-style rifle available.

Those choosing the rifle for a long-term survival gun might consider purchasing a spare firing pin and perhaps a hammer spring, ejector, and ejector spring. But the chance of needing any spare parts seems small if the weapon is given proper care, good ammunition is used in it, and practices like dry-firing are avoided.

For the poor souls in the United States with a selective-fire Kalashnikov, auto parts could become quite hard to find thanks to the infamous 1987 legislation limiting manufacture of automatic weapons. One source of replacement parts for selective-fire versions of communist-made rifles and the Galil and Valmet is Rhino Replacement Parts, Inc. An American-made automatic

kit including hammer, sear, disconnector, and disconnector spring is available from the company for about
$99.50; a stainless-steel version is offered for $109.50.

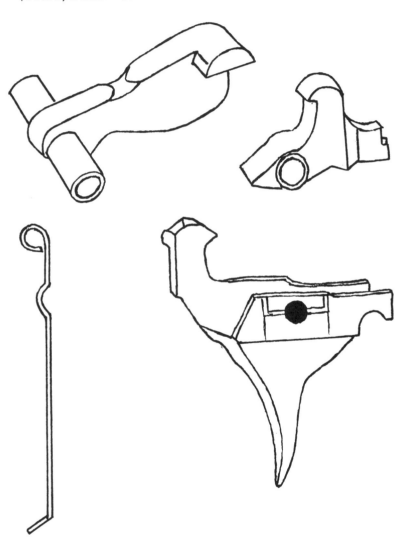

The Norinco-made, semiauto trigger group is available for
those who want spare parts for their AK. [Drawing courtesy
of Rhino Replacement Parts.]

Chinese-made automatic Norinco kits are also available for about $84.50 which will fit Norinco, Poly-Tech, and the Soviet AK47 as well as full-auto versions of the Valmet and Galil. Rhino Replacement Parts, Inc., also carries a semiauto trigger replacement group made by Norinco for around $50.00. This includes trigger, disconnector, and hammer.

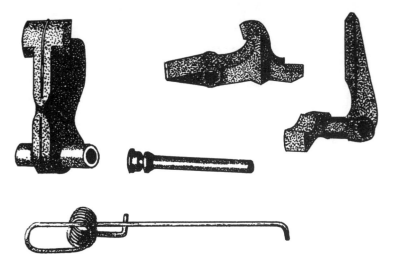

Rhino's Norinco-made, selective-fire parts including (top, left to right) hammer, disconnector, and trip pin or sear. Also shown is the cross pin and spring for the assembly. [Drawing courtesy of Rhino Replacement Parts.]

Stocks

The wooden stocks on Kalashnikovs are excellent, though some taller shooters will find some (especially the Chinese versions) a bit short. In such a case, the owner should consider using a recoil pad to add a bit of length. Those wanting to continue to use the storage compartment located in most wooden stocks can use a slip-on pad which can be quickly removed for access to the cleaning kit. Uncle Mike's makes an excellent slip-on pad available in most gun stores for under $11. The company also offers recoil spacers which can be slipped into the pad to add even more length to the rifle.

Permanent recoil pads can be used to lengthen the pull if the shooter doesn't mind sacrificing the rifle's storage compartment. Uncle Mike's offers a very fine recoil pad for less than $15, but mounting the pad, if the owner of the rifle wants it to look right, is generally a job for a gunsmith. Professional work in mounting the pad will pay off if a little time is taken to determine proper pull length for the owner of the Kalashnikov before mounting the pad.

AKM-style folding stocks leave much to be desired both in comfort and ease of operation; they tend to be a bit short and make working the safety/selector hard when the stock is folded. At the time of this writing, no one is making aftermarket folders for the Kalashnikovs, but companies like Choate Machine & Tool or others may soon offer a better folding-stock alternative.

Training/Practice .22s

While not technically an accessory, a .22 rifle modeled after the Kalashnikov can enable a shooter to gain a lot of shooting skill without spending a lot of money. Such rifles also allow practice on shooting ranges which don't accommodate high-powered rifles. These .22 rifles are also good for beginners who may be a bit noise and recoil shy.

In the United States, Mitchell Arms and EMF are currently importing Armi Jager Italian-made .22 versions of the AK-47 and Galil in both .22 LR and .22 Magnum. Outwardly, these rifles mimic the Kalashnikov's look and feel except for their lighter weight.

About the only difference between the Galil .22 and

the AK-22 is the placement of the sights, which is similar to those of the parent rifles. The .22 magazines are wider than necessary in order to give the guns the look of the centerfire rifle magazine; this also helps to keep holds from developing which are not practical with the centerfire because of its large magazines.

The .22 LR rifles use a 29-round magazine while the .22 WMR has a 10-round magazine. Stocks are made of walnut, sights are adjustable, and overall lengths are around 37 inches. Interestingly enough, the 16.5-inch barrels on the rifles give nearly maximum velocity with most .22 ammunition.

While the cost of either of these rifles approaches that of a full-size Chinese-made Kalashnikov, the money saved on less-expensive .22 ammunition will more than pay for a .22 practice rifle in a short time.

During the mid-1980s, S.W.D. of Atlanta, Georgia, made kits for converting these .22s to selective fire; these kits are no longer available, however. For a look at how the AK-22 can be converted to selective-fire use, see the January 1985 issue of *Firepower*.

• • •

The Kalashnikov is a rugged rifle with many versions affordably priced for the average shooter. The rifle is reliable to the point of being legendary, and a wealth of accessories are available for it.

Like many other rifles, the Kalashnikov has human-engineering flaws, but these can be overcome with practice or modifications. For most people who choose to carry this rifle into combat or use it for hunting or plinking, a Kalashnikov makes an ideal firearm which rarely fails when called upon to perform.

Appendix

Manufacturers and Useful Publications

MANUFACTURERS

The following companies will be of interest to those interested in or owning a Kalashnikov rifle.

Action Arms
P. O. Box 9573
Philadelphia, PA 19124
  (U.S. distributor of Galil assault rifles)

Alpha Armament
218 Main St.
Milford, OH 45150
  (Manufacturer of AK74-style muzzle brake)

Armson, Inc.
P. O. Box 2130
Farmington Hills, MI 48018
  (Distributor of OEG scopes and Trijicon rifle scopes)

Avin Industries
1847 Camino Palmero
Hollywood, CA 90046
(Distributor of LS-45 laser sights)

Brigade Quartermasters
1025 Cobb International Blvd.
Kennesaw, GA 30144-4349
(Military belts, cases, etc.,)

B-Square Company
Box 11281
Ft. Worth, TX 76110
(Manufacturer of rifle scope mounts for Kalashnikov
rifles)

Bushnell Optical Co.
2828 E. Foothill Blvd.
Pasadena, CA 91107
(Manufacturer of Banner and other model rifle and
pistol scopes)

China Sports, Inc.
4403 West Grove
Dallas, TX 75248
(Importer of Chinese NDM-86 sniper rifle)

Choate Machine & Tool
Box 218
Bald Knob, AR 72010
(Manufacturer of accessories for military-style rifles)

D.C. Brennan Firearms, Inc.
P. O. Box 2732
Cincinnati, OH 45201
(Manufacturer of Nil-Flash .223 duckbill flash
suppressor)

E and L Manufacturing, Inc.
Star Rt. 1, Box 569
Schoolhouse Road
Cave Creek, AZ 85331
(Manufacturer of AK brass catcher)

EMF Company, Inc.
1900 E. Warner Ave., Suite 1D
Santa Ana, CA 92705
(Importer of Jager AK-style .22 rifles)

Excalibur Enterprises
P. O. Box 266
Emmaus, PA 18049
(Distributor of night-vision equipment)

Fabian Bros
3333 Midway Dr., Suite 104
San Diego, CA 92110
(Distributor of DTA Mil/Brake muzzle brake/flash
hiders)

Fleming Firearms
7720 E. 126 St., N.
Collinsville, OK 74021
(Distributor of modified Chinese AKM rifles including
Mini-47)

Gun Parts
West Hurley, NY 12491
  (Dealer of military surplus equipment and rifle parts)

Hansen Cartridge Company
244 Old Post Rd.
Southport, CT 06490
  (Importer of 5.56mm NATO, 7.62x39mm, and other
  non-corrosive foreign-made ammunition)

Hodgdon Powder Company, Inc.
6231 Robinson, P. O. Box 2932
Shawnee Mission, KS 66201
  (Manufacturer of smokeless powder)

J. C. Manufacturing, Inc.
1173 Osborne Road
Spring Lake Park, MN 55432
  (Manufacturer of M203 PI grenade launcher for
  Kalashnikov rifles)

Jones Optical Company
6367 Arapahoe Rd.
Boulder, CO 80303
  (Manufacturer of polycarbonate sunglasses and combat
  goggles)

Kassnar Imports, Inc.
P. O. Box 6097
Harrisburg, PA 17112
  (Importer of semiauto AKMs)

Keng's Firearms Specialty, Inc.
P. O. Box 1176
Riverdale, GA 30274-1176
  (Importer of Chinese-made Kalashnikovs and
  accessories)

Kimel Industries, Inc.
P. O. Box 335
Matthews, NC 28105
  (Importer of Chinese semiauto Kalashnikovs)

Litton
Electron Tube Div.
1215 S. 52nd. St.
Tempe, AZ 85281
  (Manufacturer of night-vision equipment)

Magnum Research, Inc.
7271 Commerce Circle West
Minneapolis, MN 55432
  (One-time importer of Galil assault rifles; importer of
  Nimrod Galil scopes)

Michaels of Oregon Company ("Uncle Mike's")
P. O. Box 13010
Portland, OR 97213
  (Manufacturer of excellent nylon belts, pouches, slings,
  and rifle cases)

Mitchell Arms Co.
116 East 16th St.
Costa Mesa, CA 92627
  (Importer of Galil and AK47 .22 LR "lookalikes")

Navy Arms Company Inc.
689 Bergen Blvd.
Ridgefield, NJ 07657
   (Importer of Chinese Kalashnikov-style air rifles,
   AKMs, and accessories)

Pacific International Merchandising Corp.
2215 J Steet
Sacramento, Ca 95816
   (Importer of Chinese semiauto Kalashnikovs)

PMC (Patton and Morgan Corp.)
4890 S. Alameda
Los Angeles, CA 90058-2806
   (Importer of low-cost, Korean-made military-style rifle
   cartridges and .22 ammunition)

Poly Technologies, Inc.
4 New Spring Rd., Suite 340
Atlanta, GA 30339
   (U.S. branch of Chinese military industries)

Ram-Line, Inc.
15611 W. 6th Ave.
Golden, CO 80401
   (Manufacturer of rifle accessories including plastic
   bipod)

Rhino Replacement Parts, Inc.
P.O. Box 669
Seneca, SC 29679
   (Replacement parts, muzzle brakes, and scope mounts
   for AK rifles. Catalog $2)

Sherwood International Export Corp.
18714 Parthenia St.
Northridge, CA 91324
  (Distributor of military accessories, surplus parts and
  equipment)

Sierra Supply
P. O. Box 1390
Durango, CO 81301
  (Surplus dealer of military cleaning kits, AK magazine
  pouches, and other military equipment)

Smith Enterprises
325 South Westwood #1
Mesa, AZ 85202
  (Manufacturer of Vortex duckbill-style flash
  suppressor)

Standard Equipment Company
9240 N. 107th St.
Milwaukee, WI 53224
  (Distributor of night-vision equipment)

Stoeger Industries
55 Ruta Ct.
S. Hackensack, NJ 07606
  (U.S. importers of the Valmet rifles)

Tasco
3625 NW 82nd Ave., Suite 310
Miami, FL 33166
  (Manufacturer of rifle and pistol scopes)

Territorial Armory
4455 South Park, Suite 106
Tucson, AZ 85714
(Distributor of Poly Technology Chinese-made rifles
and accessories)

Traders Sports, Inc.
685 E. 14th St.
San Leandro, CA 94577
(Importer of Yugoslavian semiauto rifles)

USEFUL PUBLICATIONS

The following books and magazines have valuable information which will be of interest to those needing more information about similar small arms, new weapons developments, ammunition, and other subjects related to the Kalashnikov rifles.

The AK47 Story
By Edward Clinton Ezell
Stackpole Books
Cameron and Kelker Streets, P. O. Box 1831
Harrisburg, PA 17105

American Rifleman Magazine
1600 Rhode Island Ave., NW
Washington, DC 20036

American Survival Guide Magazine
McMullen Publishing
P. O. Box 15690
Santa Ana, CA 92705-0690

Assault Pistols, Rifles and Submachine Guns
By Duncan Long
Paladin Press
P. O. Box 1307
Boulder, CO 80306

Combat Ammunition
By Duncan Long
Paladin Press
P. O. Box 1307
Boulder, CO 80306

Firepower Magazine
Turbo Publishing
P. O. Box 518
Cottonwood, AZ 86326

S.W.A.T. Magazine
148 South Main St.
Cottonwood, AZ 86326

Terrorist Weapons Course #92 (AK47 rifles)
Allied Books
P. O. Box 5070
Glendale, AZ 85312